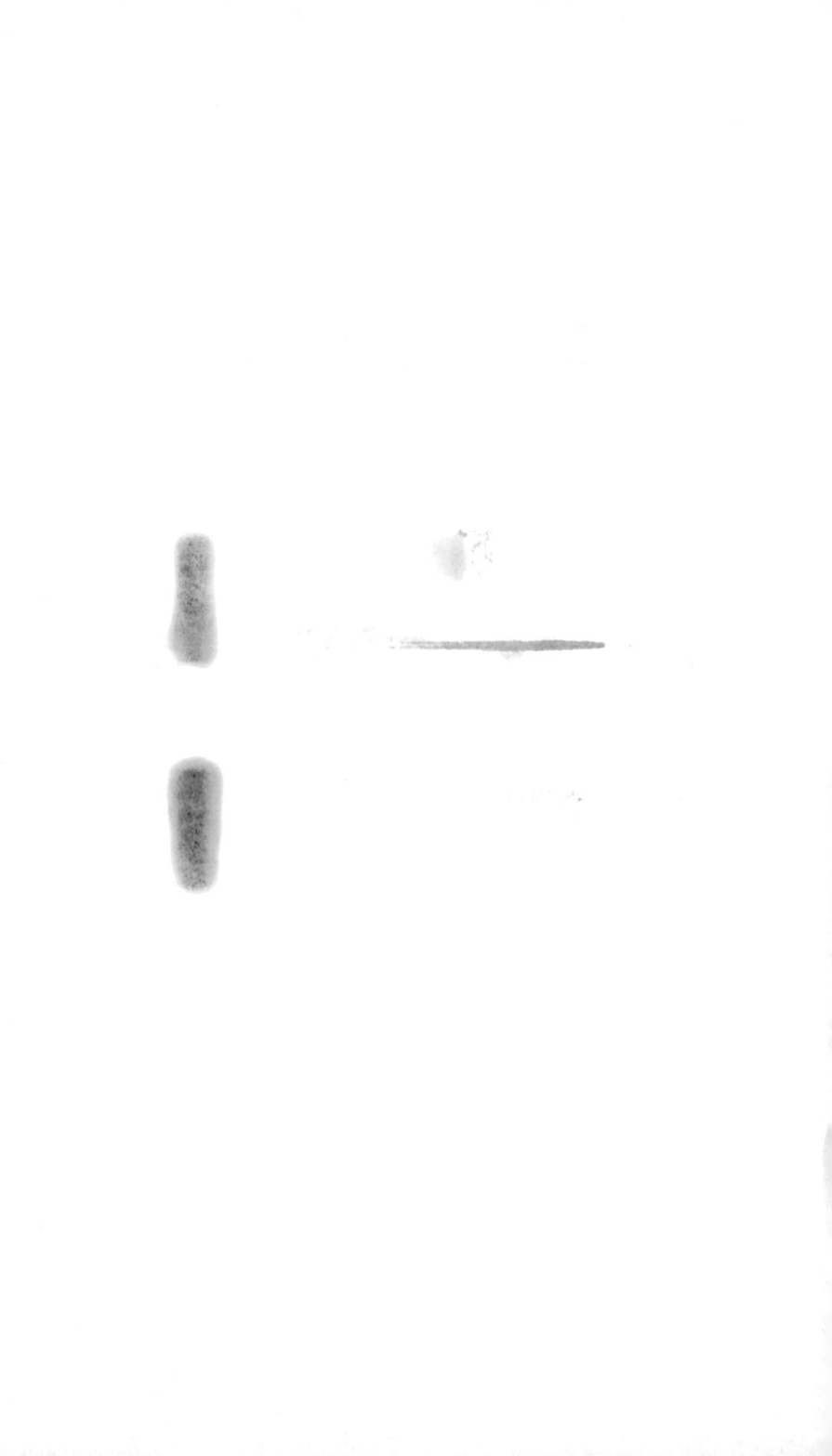

Knowing God?

Consumer Christianity and the Gospel of Jesus

Michael Hardin

FOREWORD BY
Chris Tilling

CASCADE *Books* • Eugene, Oregon

KNOWING GOD?
Consumer Christianity and The Gospel of Jesus

Copyright © 2020 Michael Hardin. All rights reserved. Except for brief quotations in critical publications or reviews, no part of this book may be reproduced in any manner without prior written permission from the publisher. Write: Permissions, Wipf and Stock Publishers, 199 W. 8th Ave., Suite 3, Eugene, OR 97401.

Cascade Books
An Imprint of Wipf and Stock Publishers
199 W. 8th Ave., Suite 3
Eugene, OR 97401

www.wipfandstock.com

PAPERBACK ISBN: 978-1-5326-8389-3
HARDCOVER ISBN: 978-1-5326-8390-9
EBOOK ISBN: 978-1-5326-8391-6

Cataloguing-in-Publication data:

Names: Hardin, Michael, author. | Tilling, Chris, foreword.

Title: Knowing God? : consumer Christianity and the gospel of Jesus / by Michael Hardin ; foreword by Chris Tilling.

Description: Eugene, OR: Cascade Books, 2020 | Includes bibliographical references.

Identifiers: ISBN 978-1-5326-8389-3 (paperback) | ISBN 978-1-5326-8390-9 (hardcover) | ISBN 978-1-5326-8391-6 (ebook)

Subjects: LCSH: Atonement. | Peace—Religious aspects—Christianity.

Classification: BT265.3 .H35 2020 (print) | BT265.3 (ebook)

Manufactured in the U.S.A.   05/15/20

Dedicated to

My Love, My Angel, Lorri

Who more than any other has shown me who Jesus is

And to

All the bandmates of Yes

Whose music has saved my life and nurtured my heart time and again

"Change We Must To Live Again"

~Jon Anderson

And just because this is my book and I can:

"Go Big Blue!"

Contents

Foreword by Chris Tilling | ix
Preface | xiii
Introduction | xv

CHAPTER 1   Consumer Christianity and Christian Spirituality | 1

CHAPTER 2   Mysticism | 10

CHAPTER 3   Crucifixion | 26

CHAPTER 4   Resurrection | 38

CHAPTER 5   Ascension | 48

CHAPTER 6   Incarnation | 62

CHAPTER 7   Conclusion: A Two Chart Primer On How To Read The Bible | 76

Resources from Michael Hardin | 87

Foreword

When Michael Hardin asked me to write the foreword to this book, I rather impulsively agreed without having read any of his published work. What would I say if I didn't like it?! Sure, I've enjoyed the times we have chatted over Skype and felt energized by his obvious passion and learning. But a book is another matter entirely.

So I was in the same situation as you right now: I didn't know what to expect.

But as I dipped my toes into Hardin's literary waters, it quickly became apparent that I was writing a foreword to a book of flames. Hardin wrote this book as a prophet with fire in his bones.

And that, I submit, is the key to reading this book. The short volume you hold in your hands now isn't best read as an instruction manual or a dispassionate textbook. This is a book written to disturb, stir, and refocus. This is, in other words, a short and sharp book; it's combustible. It's a concentrated ginger shot. It's a hot sauce gumball. It's a quick-working enema tablet. It's a cold shower. It's a Chinese burn of a book.

Like the prophet gazing into the heavens and hearing that his descendants will be as numerous as the sand on the seashore, or like the other prophet (Isaiah) who spoke of mountains melting in blood, or like the time Jesus said that not one stone would remain on another... they were not best heard as if presenting mere factual claims, as if they were dishing out dull propositions to be dissected by a logic-chopping computer program. Likewise, Hardin's book is written to jolt us out of our complicity with idolatrous versions of Christianity. It is injected with prophetic passion and insight, and so should be read accordingly.

This means that it's written for a particular audience. It is for those who are despondent with what has passed as Christianity in the West, yet hopeful that the good news might still be truly good. It's written for those who are tired of a faith cast against the backdrop of a rather ominous and angry god whose finger is just hovering over a smite button because of our sins. Michael writes for those burdened and weighed down with a sense that god dislikes them, burned out by a deity who wants—no, demands—more obedience from your pathetic, lazy, compromising ass before he can start properly to love you.

But this book is also penned for those bored with the Jesus who apparently likes it when we self-righteously call other people Nazis. It's written for those who have been told that your gender or skin color disqualifies your voice. It's a hot condemnation of all that gives the impression that only avocado latte-drinking hipsters who hitch their cart to the latest woke political causes are truly "in."

Hardin argues that all of these tired, legalistic, and boring versions of Christianity are merely stalls in something called the "Christian Religious Shopping Mall." They are forms of Christianity unhinged from the cross of Christ, and as such do obeisance at the feet of some kind of human religious projection, not the God revealed in Jesus Christ. Whether they end up with a feel-good god or a tyrant god, they have effectively displaced Jesus Christ.

Hardin's words are thus thunder and lightning, railing against Shopping Mall Christianity, but precisely because he confronts us with the true offense of the cross. "Were you there when they crucified my Lord?" "Yes!" exclaims Hardin, and we were part of that crowd calling for the death of God. And right there, where we were exposed at our worst, God announces that unilateral and complete forgiveness. As Hardin writes: "In Jesus' death we are all found as forgiven persecutors." This is the strange way of God revealed in the cross, which brings all economies of exchange with God to an end. It is the good news that God forgives all, completely and fully, not when we repent, not when we believe, not . . . add your condition. God has *forgiven*! Period. And this is what makes faith and repentance good news.

Hardin captures what is at the heart of Pauline theology with this, explaining that in the resurrection of Christ, we are all made brothers and sisters of Christ. The story of Jesus Christ, his death and resurrection, isn't a story back then and over there. It *is* our story. We die with Christ and are raised with Christ, as Paul so powerfully put it in his letters. Exactly those calling for the death of God find themselves to be made his beloved family.

And Michael is clear that we are also included in the risen and ascended Jesus' *ongoing* ministry at the right hand of God. Christ, our Great High Priest, is our ongoing human relationship with God. Or, as other theologians have put it, he is our human "Yes" to God. We don't need to be frightened by our own spiritual ineptitude, in other words, for that would merely perpetuate the narcissism of consumer Christianity. We are not turned in on ourselves but rather enfolded into the love of God revealed in the life, death, resurrection, and ascension of Jesus Christ.

So while this book is a profound and scorching indictment of contemporary "consumer Christianity," it is so because it presents us with a delighted and dynamic vision of Jesus, one that draws on deep theological and biblical wells. Hardin writes about life for all in the crucified and risen Christ, and for this reason some will come away with burnt fingers, with pious religious projections uncermoniously scattered across the floor. But it is my prayer that you will rather come away with warmed hearts, energized by the wonderful news revealed in Jesus Christ, a life which is truly for all, and about which Michael Hardin writes with such clarity.

Chris Tilling
On the feast day of St Mellitus,
April 24, 2019

Preface

Every book ever written has a history, a back story, and is also engaged in a debate with previously written books or viewpoints. This is especially true in the modern era. There is a tendency among readers in the Christian churches to read books apart from awareness of the background and culture of the authors. But books cannot be lifted out of history. Thus we do not read the writings of St. Francis the same way we read those of Dietrich Bonhoeffer. Each was writing for their own contemporaries in their own time.

So too this book has a back story and is engaged in contemporary debates about Christianity, the message of the gospel and the character of God. The author was raised Roman Catholic in America but like a lot of youth got converted to Protestantism, forty-three years ago. It has not been a happy conversion for either Protestantism or myself. For those two-score-plus decades I have been a pilgrim wandering about Protestantism in America. I have attended churches that were conservative, fundamentalist, evangelical, liberal, progressive, emergent, Charismatic, pacifist (in theory), militant, just to name a few. And in these forty-three years I have yet to find a congregation that has actually learned to live into the message of Jesus.

And I am stupefied by this. How is it that Jesus is so different from Christianity? What happened to make this so? What is really wrong with Christianity? More to the point, how can we even know the answers to these questions? And finally, how does the good news of Jesus and about Jesus set us free? How can we be as authentically human as Jesus? These are the questions I am pursuing in this book.

I want to thank Andrew Hammer for providing me coffee resources while I was writing this manuscript. To Kathy, Tammy, Lori, and Jen, thanks for serving me in my other office at Alice's. I am also grateful to my friends, especially Greg Vadala and David Grant, for standing with me during "The Troubles." Thanks are also proffered to Keith Hayes, Grant Dean, David Roberts, Brian van Tubergen, Simone Rammaci, Wendy Francisco, Adolphe Mboumte, Daniel Essaka, and my other friends and "students" in the Classroom of the Dude of Theology, for their support and encouragement as we pursue Jesus as a deer pants for the water brook.

May Jesus always be your light.

Michael Hardin
Easter 2019

Introduction

Life is not lived in a box. Real life, full orbed in-your-face life, is a roller coaster ride, a medieval quest on steroids, a full throttle adventure. Real life is not cookie-cutter existence. Around every bend there is a surprise waiting.

Sometimes surprises are quite fun, like birthday parties. We jump with joy.

Sometimes surprises are deadly, like poisonous insects or snakes. We jump in fear.

No matter how you slice it or dice it, life is full of surprises. We simply cannot know the future; nor can we control all of the various factors that make up our present. We can try, but just ask any mother how crazy a day can go when one little thing jams up the day and everything else in its wake tumbles into everything else. By nighttime, as the weary body hits the bed and the lights go out, there is barely room to breathe and one is hanging by the last emotional thread, only to realize that the alarm has been set so that tomorrow this thing called "life" can be done all over again.

And again. And again. Life can feel like an endless repetition of circling dead ends and leave us wondering if we somehow missed the train of "meaning and purpose" at the station.

Who are we anyway? Does it matter? Is this thing we do called life, life?

Now we all come from somewhere. By this I mean we all have life experiences that have shaped the way we see the world or imagine the future. No two of us are the same in this. Yet we do share some commonalities that allow us to communicate across the vast expanse of our complex and diverse life experiences. I do not know you, or at least I do not yet know you. However, if you are reading this you may already know something about me. You may know some basic facts: I am married to Lorri, have daughters and granddaughters, live in Pennsylvania, have attended seminary, like classic rock and roll, and enjoy traveling, speaking to groups, and meeting new people. I love reading books and listening to music and writing theology. The natural world, birds and trees and rocks and water, sunsets and forests, wind, rain, and sun delight me. You can infer from some of these facts certain things but you still wouldn't know me.

Unless I further revealed myself.

You then might learn how each night I "let go" of the disastrous surprises of each day.

How I think about my family and give thanks for them.

Or that I often fall asleep praying.

I'm not saying that prayer is boring. Not at all. At least I don't find my own prayers boring, for they are a recital before God of who I am, where I am at, how I feel and what I think. And in turn they are often a reflection of how I understand the presence of God in my everyday, rather routine existence, from waking up and having coffee, to meeting with Lorri, reading, writing, engaging others, taking care of administrative tasks, helping my granddaughters with their homework (except for math or science, which I just don't get), to cooking dinner, writing on Facebook, checking emails, and maybe watching something interesting on the telly with Lorri. Nothing to see here, folks, move along. In other words, I live a life just the same as you do. We all have our routines.

For some people routines are a rut.

Same old, same old. Boring. Life for them feels like an endless repetition of walking a treadmill to nowhere.

For some people routines are a ritual.

Rituals can be very meaningful. They can give structure to an otherwise chaotic existence. I have a lot of positive things to say about ritual. Until ritual becomes an OCD thing. Then routines experienced as rituals are fearsome, for unless they are practiced perfectly and correctly life cannot be properly balanced.

Finally, for some people routines are a groove.

Yes, they bring structure and purpose to ordering the day. However, they are not ends in themselves. Traveling in a groove suggests that life is actually going somewhere, like water flowing in an aqueduct, or a needle playing music off an album. I am so old school I know. But think about it. Back in the 1960s and 1970s those of us hippie types who were having a most excellent time would say that life was "groovy." By this we understood that life just flowed along and sometimes it would go left and sometimes it would go right, sometimes life would speed up and sometimes it would slow down. But it was life and we experienced it as a groove, not a rut. In those days everything was "groovy."

People with gray hair are grinning from ear to ear right now. They know exactly what I am talking about.

The reason I bring up this business of life, and surprises and routines, is that, for many, the practice of faith has become dull, or boring or senseless. Out of this dullness and boredom many have searched to recapture the surprise that life offers. So they have sought out the new, the extraordinary, the supernatural, or that which was different, the latest fad or craze, the most out-of-the-box experience they could find.

They read books by people whose life experience seemed far out there. They looked up to the famous, the wealthy, and the bizarre. And a new form of Christianity was born.

Consumer Christianity. A Christianity designed to meet your every whim, wish, and desire. A Christianity that promised salvation through a genie in a bottle, a miracle cure, or a new divine revelation. A Christianity, they said, that would knock your socks off; complete with kitsch for every room of your house and every nook and cranny of your soul. Oh, this Christianity promised power, wealth, fame and fortune, health, glory, and stupendous downloads from the Divine Supercomputer in the Sky.

It came by ways of tents, then small buildings with white picket fences. It came by way of radio, then television. It came by way of mega ministries, nattily dressed pastors preening like peacocks and telethons, DVDs, downloads, and finally, the Internet. It came as a flash flood at the end of the twentieth century. Consumer Christianity promised it all.

It delivered nothing.

It was bankrupt and empty.

In the end, the spiritual mall that is Consumer Christianity, with all of its promises and gimmicks, deceptions and abuses, sales and discounted merchandise, has become a toxic zone, a wasteland. In the memorable words of theologian Dietrich Bonhoeffer, who died at the hands of the Nazis in 1945, Consumer Christianity is just another marketplace for "cheap grace."

Cheap grace is found in many forms. It always involves one of these three major components and in worst-case scenarios all three: illusion, self-deception, and affirmation of the status quo.

This Consumer Christianity has a wife: Empire. It has always been a married duo, from the time of Constantine in the fourth century until the present. Consumer Christianity is Empire Christianity, it is a religion that caters to the masses, but feeds them empty calories, offers poisonous water to drink, uses, abuses and confuses people.

And it has done its job very well, this false religion masquerading as Christianity. It spreads faster than flu, is as deadly as Ebola, and is difficult to treat once caught.

It now infects our entire planet. Consumer Christianity is killing us.

However, it is not only the virus that is out there. There is an antidote that has been injected into the human consciousness, an antidote that in various times and places has taken hold, has gripped the imagination, and has been a prophetic voice in the wilderness. This antidote is the gospel story about Jesus.

But "Wait," you say. "Isn't Consumer Christianity about Jesus?"

The answer is yes and no.

Yes, in the sense that it uses his name. No, in the sense that the Jesus that is represented is not at all about Jesus of Nazareth. Jesus, as he is talked about in Consumer Christianity, is a fake.

INTRODUCTION

The "real" Jesus, the one who lived historically and is seated at the right hand of God, is the Jesus we seek to know, for it is this Jesus who offers us a path to life that is profoundly different than the dead ends and roads to nowhere of Consumer Christianity. It is this Jesus we seek to know and whose life we seek to emulate and ultimately whose life is lived in us.

From this point on in the rest of this book we are going to do some thinking together about God. I will seek to be as clear as possible and I don't want to burden this book with footnotes or Bible quotes. I wrote a slightly scholarly book about this in 2010 titled *The Jesus Driven Life*. That book has more than 375 footnotes and references. This book does not. For those who wish to understand more about how I understand Jesus, that is the book to consult. And further resources for this way of thinking are found at the end of this book. This was written in a different style. It is written for you.

CHAPTER 1

Consumer Christianity and Christian Spirituality

Life has always had it challenges, but it seems to me that there are extra challenges we face today that were unknown to our parents and grandparents. One of those challenges is the challenge of meaning. What do our lives mean? What do we mean?

What does anything mean?

In a world where every opinion seems to have a conflicting opinion or six, where talk, language, news, and chats are given spin, where disinformation abounds, how can we know what anything means? If we have trouble knowing what anything means where can we find truth?

"What is truth?" In truth, do not we all share Pilate's question?

Ever since the time of the European Reformation (sixteenth century) this has also been a question asked by Protestants. Was it the Catholic Church that had the truth? Or was it Martin Luther and his churches? Perhaps it was John Calvin and his church in Geneva. Or maybe truth was to be found in the marginal sects of Anabaptists who sought to practice the Sermon on the Mount. Who knew then and who knows now where truth is to be found? When you add the world-changing effects of the philosophy of

René Descartes and the rise of secular modernity to this, not to mention the influence of figures like John Wesley or the Puritan writers, and you multiply this by 400 years of clashes, conflicts, and wars between churches and between science and theology, it is little wonder that the twenty-first century just feels like an enormous QUESTION MARK.

Of course I am only speaking of the Western church; we have not even gotten around to looking at the problems of the Eastern churches!

Add to this mix of questions even more "churchy" questions related to authority. Who is authorized to tell the truth? Is it the church proper? Is it the pope? Or maybe the bishops? Maybe it was the great Creeds or perhaps it was one of the numerous Protestant Confessions. Or maybe it is the totally relevant hipster in jeans that is so cool? Or could it be that truth was to be found in a collection of books which was "really one book" because it "really had one author"? I speak of the Bible of course.

Over the past 500 years every single one of these has been claimed as THE source for THE truth and every single one of these sources has been examined and found wanting, for a variety of reasons. Of course, there are still those who will argue about and for each one of these, but fewer and fewer people are willing to trust anything completely or give final authority to another, even to "a" book.

We have lived through 500 years of arguing. Many times that arguing has turned ugly. For thirty years in the seventeenth century it became open warfare, otherwise known as the Thirty Years War that decimated Europe. It is becoming open conflict in my contemporary United States of America.

This warfare has become open among families and between spouses. Dare I mention social media? One benefit of the Internet is that it has exposed, for all to see, our collective human ignorance.

Furious battles rage and sides are taken over the minutest discussions. These discussions are chaired by people who actually think they know something when they know so very precious little. It is not only misinformation that abounds on the Internet, it is stupidity. All of the Christians get on the Internet and try to convince the others to go to the Mall of Empire Christianity and shop at their favorite store, while those who have a favorite store (for all Christians do) try to find reasons *not* to shop at that *other* store.

But let's admit it: there has been an awful lot of arguing over the pettiest of details, the smallest of differences. Once in awhile these differences might actually make a difference, but most of the time they don't.

Why?

Because they are differences *within* the Empire of Consumer Christianity.

These theological differences are like selecting from among fifty different brands of toilet tissue. They all do the same thing in my experience, some more comfortably than others (and who in the world invented single-ply tissue?). But they are all the same thing essentially. So it is with the religious differences so many people argue about. Since these differences are all within the Empire of Consumer Christianity there is really no substantive difference between them.

Within the Empire of Consumer Christianity you are free to shop at any one of 40,000+ stores for your particular brand of spiritual experience. Every store you go in will claim that their experience is the best and that they have no rivals. Some of the more expensive stores will cost you an arm and a leg but will promise you a spiritual experience that is out of body and out of mind. However, in the long run, after you have shopped there all you really are is out of money.

Modern Christianity has become little more than a religious shopping mall. Even church architecture is moving in this direction, complete with coffee bars, gift shops, and now, horror of horrors, McDonald's! What is on offer in the Empire of Consumer Christianity, no matter what church you enter, is really the same old thing. It is just packaged differently. It is the packaging that matters. Churches, ministries, and pastors all fight over their packaging, each contending that it is their packaging that is inspired by God. But when you open the package you get the same old dysfunctional religion every time.

Why is this?

I would like to suggest, following a line of thinking by my friend Jon Pahl, that the Empire of Consumer Christianity is just a replication (archetype perhaps?) of the regular shopping mall experience designed to get you to empty your wallets. Religion has always been about money and power. There is no denying this fact, especially as one explores the origins of human religion. Religion begins and ends with fear: fear of life and fear of death.

This should not come as a surprise. Religion and the modern economy have similar functions. I do not wish to get too technical, but in order for us to understand the commercialization of modern Christianity it is important for us to grasp that the mechanism that underlies our economy and that of religion is identical. It is called an "economy of exchange."

Let me offer an example. The only really valuable "thing" you possess in your life that you can exchange for something else is your time. When that alarm clock rings you set about exchanging your time for a paycheck. You can then exchange that paycheck for "money" (virtual or real) and then you can exchange that money for goods and services.

Your time becomes valuable. You can augment your time and make it more valuable by getting an education. Education gains you a set of skills that make you more valuable to an employer. That exchange of your time (years of college and/or more years of a post-graduate education) also comes with a cost, either in student loans or debt (or both!). The goal in the long run is to make an exchange of time that will create greater value for you so your paycheck will be larger and you have more purchasing power.

This is how we have ended up in a culture where net worth equals self-worth.

The same thing is occurring in the Empire of Consumer Christianity.

In those churches they tell you that God requires you to give money in order to get a blessing. God will not bless you until you "sow into the ministry." These same churches also tell people that they need to be there every time the doors are open. God cannot do anything with you unless you are a full-on participant. One pastor recently refused to bury a woman who had been two years in a coma because "she had not been a recent tither."

The god of the Empire of Consumer Christianity requires something from you before he will do anything for you.

Where does this kind of thinking stem from?

It comes from a belief in a god who is a heavenly accountant, a bookkeeper. This god is like Santa Claus, keeping lists of who's naughty and nice.

This god gets angry at people who do not conform to a set of expectation or rules.

This god requires sacrifices in order to placate wrath and anger.

This god needs life, our life, our sweat, blood, and tears, in order to exist. Deny these and this god ceases to exist. Preachers know this, some consciously, most non-consciously. So it is that week after week they dun their congregations with rules and regulations, expectations and promises of judgment if they do not or will not conform.

This repeated dunning of regular folks in the pews has caused a reaction in Empire of Consumer Christianity. People have stopped coming to the Mall. People are fleeing churches. Many people have turned to atheism or agnosticism. They have rejected a god who is no different than their tyrannical boss, their demanding spouse, or their parents.

What is fascinating is how many people then turn to "feel good" preachers who are also caught up in the Empire of Consumer Christianity but take advantage of those who have been abused by the Tyrant God.

These preachers offer a thinly veiled "success story" of how when they rejected the Tyrant God for the loving God they began to be successful. They walk onto a stage in their three-piece suits and tell you that God wants you to be as successful as they have become. God wants you to have an inspiring ministry just like theirs. God wants you to have supernatural power or some secret insight just like they do.

These preachers claim that if you will "give" to their ministry these secrets of success will be yours. Now, most people, having to choose between the Tyrant God and a loving God, will choose the latter. So when preachers promise healing or success or secrets or keys, people will gladly pay through the nose. Just like when they were stuck in churches that debased them and took their money so now they are stuck in a religious economy of exchange that makes them feel good . . . at a price.

They have fled the Tyrant god for the Feel Good god when both end up being the same thing. You see, these kinds of churches are all run like pyramid schemes. There is only so much room at the top. You can be successful, just not more successful than the one at the top. You can do supernatural miracles, just not more than the one at the top. You can teach secrets or keys to success just as long as you are not more successful than the ones above you in the hierarchy.

Just as pyramid schemes promise you the world if you will work hard enough, prospect long enough, and get enough people to join you in your venture, so also preachers in the Empire of Consumer Christianity tell you the same. They offer as proof their own "success" story. They claim God has blessed them and if you will imitate their experience, you too will be able to have all the supernatural life, money, power, fame, and fortune that they do.

However, the burn-out stories of those who have done this are as replete as those who have left the Tyrant God. In both cases, deity is still being conceived in an economy of exchange. God needs proof before God does anything. God needs your money, your faith, your good works, your time, and your sacrifices before God will do anything for you. If you believe this, I have a bridge in Brooklyn you can buy!

A small franchise became an anchor store in the Mall of Consumer Christianity this past several years. It is called Movement. It has identity politics as its merchandise. While this store, unlike its competitors, purchases fair trade products and has a fairer compensation plan for its employees than other stores in the Mall, the bottom line is that its products are just as illusory as those found in other stores. Identity politics is structured like an indoor flea market, and here any two people that can form a group from something they share in common a booth. It is a bit chaotic in this store, inasmuch as there is a constant vying for the best spots and every booth owner swears that their identity is most important. Sometimes fist fights among the vendors break out in this store.

But in the long run this store is just like all the other stores in the Mall. It is a store. Most of the time those who sell their products here plot ways to go rob the other stores! Consumer Christianity may be married to Empire but she has been having a torrid affair with Calvinist capitalism and Marxist atheism (depending on whether you are conservative or liberal). This illicit ménage a trois is the reason we are where we are.

Authentic Christian identity is not found, it is given and that by God. The Mall seduces you with its alluring advertisements about how unfulfilled you are, how unhappy you are, how unworthy you are until you come and shop with them. The Mall seeks to be that which when asked, answers; when sought, is found. It exudes hospitality and will open its doors to anyone who knocks.

NEWS FLASH!

The god of the Empire of Consumer Christianity isn't real.

This god does not exist except in the vain imaginations of people. And these vain imaginations often turn dark and ugly. This is especially so when the Mall begins to lose customers.

I know this will be a terrible bother to some, but it needs to be said. Religion will do anything, including killing its own prophets, in order to survive.

Now what I am saying is not new, in fact it is ancient, as ancient as the Jewish prophets, as ancient as Jesus of Nazareth. Speaking truth to power, especially religious power, can and often does get one demoted, ostracized, demonized, or ultimately scapegoated.

BUT . . . whether speaking to power or money, truth will not stand idly by, watching while religion eats away at the heart of humanity.

CHAPTER 2

Mysticism

If you happen to be in a bookstore right now and are browsing this book to see if you wish to purchase it, look at some of the other titles on the shelves. Notice how those titles promise health, wealth, and success and that they offer the "keys" to this or the "secrets" to that or the "ways" to something else.

KEYS! SECRETS! SOMETHING YOU DO NOT POSSESS BUT CAN PURCHASE!

AND TODAY LIVING THE CHRISTIAN LIFE IS 30 PERCENT OFF.

Each of these books is making a promise that if you purchase that book and follow the formula therein you too, like the author, will be assured of achieving your dreams and reaching your goals. You will have a Lamborghini life.

Dreams and goals are laudable. Without them we would remain in the ruts I spoke about earlier. When you were a child, do recall adults asking you what you wanted to be when you grew up? Sure you do. We ask the same thing from our own children from time to time. We seek to help them aspire to something, to think outside the box. If we are wise we teach our children how to formulate realistic goals that are measurable and achievable. We can encourage them to dream and to dream big.

There is nothing wrong with any of that as long as you are in a position to help your children and are willing to do what it takes to be a coach, cheerleader, and shoulder to cry on when the inevitable failures occur.

Here is the thing: there are no guarantees in life. One may practice a skill until fingers bleed or minds ache, and one may still not become top tier or make the final cut.

Life is full of disappointments, of unrealized expectations, and of frustrated dreams. Just ask all those with PhDs who cannot find work in their chosen field and instead are flipping hamburgers at McDonald's or working at Home Depot (and these two examples are both friends of mine).

Now the Empire of Consumer Christianity has ways to get you to buy your dreams from them. Notice I said "buy your dreams," because these big visions of life do not come cheap. They have a thousand ways to convince you that you need the church and all of its many colored programs in order to succeed and live "the successful Christian life."

However, that isn't the worst part of it. If, after you have shopped at the Mall of Consumer Christianity, and you cannot find what you are looking for, there is a store, a giant retail outlet called the Shop of Mystical Wonders. As you wander inside, strobe lights flash all manner of psychedelic promises, music surrounds you in deep luxurious bass tones and soul-piercing trebles, display after display of anecdotal fashions adorn the aisles as you wend your way through this amazing and majestic wonderland.

At last!

You have found what you are looking for, the promise of an intimate encounter with the Divine.

What more could you ask for than your very own personal relationship with God?

Yes, you too can be the owner of the grand prize, your very own share in this stock, given from heaven and dispensed only here in this store. Look at the sales people with that happy glow on their faces and the store manager who delightfully shows consumers how they can find the perfect mix-and-match mystical ensemble. Why, there are even fads and fashions from foreign markets!

Who can resist such glitz?

You can accessorize your purchases with special event sales (called seminars or ministry schools) and receive all the latest new-fangled experiences available. Some of them are even being beta tested right here in the store.

So, once again you pull out your credit card and gleefully hand it over so that you too may partake in this cutting-edge, fashionable experience.

Cha-ching! Thank you very much.

Mysticism is a big money-making business today. Long before the Empire of Consumer Christianity got into it, the 1960s hippie radicals were finding out all about it through LSD and Indian gurus. How did we arrive at such a place where the odd, the bizarre, and the utterly strange became the norm for spiritual experience?

It begins long before the 1950s. But if you know a little about the post-World War II church-cultural situation in America then you can understand the reaction of the 1960s, the Jesus Movement and the stepchildren of that movement, notably found in certain charismatic Christian circles.

The 1950s were the heyday of the institutional churches, the big denominations like the Lutherans, the Methodists, and the growing movements of Evangelicalism and Fundamentalism. Pete Seeger sang about "ticky-tacky houses all in a row" and the same thing could have been said about the churches of that time. Everything about church life at that time was neat and orderly. People dressed in their Sunday best and America was a fine upstanding nation following the great victory of the war. Business boomed. Suburbs came into being and with those suburbs came white flight.

Then the cancerous division aggressively grew.

Forty-thousand-plus different denominations would eventually register with the US government as a "religious non-profit," each one presuming it had some angle or corner on the truth the other churches in town did not have. Think about this: there are over 4,000 different types of Baptists.

Four thousand!

Little wonder that Doctrine Wars are the norm. Every denomination sought to preserve their identity by appealing to the past, to their founders, and to their confessions of faith. The Christian life was about believing the right thing. Evangelicals reacted strongly against what they perceived as the liberalism of mainline Christianity and mainline churches reacted against the myopic vision and paranoia of Evangelicalism and Fundamentalism.

Then the 1960s exploded on the scene. The space race and the Beatles, the civil rights movement, Viet Nam, drugs, the importation of eastern religious philosophies, the God-is-dead movement. JFK, Bobby Kennedy, Malcolm X, and Martin Luther King, Jr., were all assassinated. There was Woodstock and then Watergate. The comfortable 1950s gave way to the tumultuous 1960s.

The Roman Catholic Church sought to change and the fresh winds of Vatican II blew through her open windows. The ecumenical movement and dialogues of the mainline churches were in full swing. The divide between the "conservative" Evangelical, Fundamentalist, and Independent churches and the "liberal" mainline traditions grew greater year by year. People sought for constancy in a culture that was tearing itself apart.

They fled to the conservative churches. Hippies became yuppies. They traded their VW micro vans for Benzes. The inner cities, abandoned by the white middle class, became destitute and run down. Crime rates soared in the cities, while whites in the suburbs hoped crime would remain there. Conservative churches began to grow exponentially as people sought to find an oasis of stability in a world gone mad.

In the 1980s, as business flourished under the "trickle-down" economics of Ronald Reagan, so did the conservative churches. The Moral Majority was founded. The experimentation of the 1960s gave way to the despair of the 1970s, which in turn produced a "circle the wagons" mentality in Christianity in the 1980s. The success formula of big business began to be applied to church growth models. This in turn led to the rise of the mega church in the 1990s.

By the time we got to January 1, 2000, Christianity had become Big Business. It had its own industries: Christian music, Christian art, Christian entertainment, Christian movies, Christian kitsch, Christian TV and radio stations, and Christian websites. You name it and somebody baptized it as Christian, including business models. It had become a mall.

Pastors became CEOs, people became numbers, politely called "customers." Sure, some customers would leave but there were always new customers that could be attracted with the proper marketing.

All this time the Empire of Consumer Christianity was busying itself with creating a system that would not, could not be stopped. Christianity in America had become a "principality and power." Worse yet, American Christians were exporting this mix of business models, capitalist philosophy, corporate "bigger is better" mentality, and civil religion all over the world.

What the Empire of Consumer Christianity didn't count on was that people would tire of the legalism, the rules and regulations, the do's and don'ts, the arbitrary rulings, the bitter recriminations and the burdens of supporting an institution that felt more like a courtroom than a hospital.

People were looking for an authentic relation to the divine that was more than just prayers bouncing off ceilings.

During this whole time, a global explosion occurred that left the Evangelicals in the dust: the Charismatic movement and Pentecostalism swept through third world countries like a wildfire. The poor were attracted to a message of wealth, the sick to a message of health, the weak to a message of strength, the bored with a message of the "supernatural."

It was the seduction of the masses.

What we see today is the result of that. Third world pastors browbeat their congregations, mostly poor, to give, give, GIVE! They live in plush mansions while their congregants live in hovels. They drive their Mercedes while their parishioners walk barefoot.

The greedy sucked the needy dry.

We see the same thing here in America. When I was a pastor (a lifetime ago), I would attend clergy meetings in my denomination. When pastors gathered it was all about how big their church was, how they were growing, how much their salary was, and how big their ego (penis) was. If you happened to not fit the profile of "ladder climber," if you saw people as somehow important, if you were critical of the status quo, you were usually farmed out to small congregations where one or two families ruled the roost and all you could do was bide your time until something bigger and better came along.

The ministry is a dog-eat-dog world.

I mention all of this because I need to make clear that part of what constitutes the Empire of Consumer Christianity is that real people seeking a real relationship with God have been taken advantage of for a long time by ego-driven pastors, all out to make a name for themselves in the hopes that by so doing they could claim that God was "validating their ministry," evidenced by growth.

"I'm important, pay attention to me! I am somebody and I know more than you do anyways, pay attention to me!" "Do what I say for I have authority." "I am the true and proper interpreter of the Bible, listen to me!"

However, after eating at this table for a season of our life, many of us just went out and threw up.

All of this has contributed to the New Exodus, only this time salvation is not found within but outside the church (to reverse a saying of an ancient church father).

The rise of the groups, the "Nones" (those who claim no religious tradition) and the "Dones" (those who have had it with the church), in the United States is indicative of the reality I have just described. People have had it with fast-food religion; they seek the substantive. They are weary of quick fixes; they seek long-lasting, life-transforming solutions. Too many are no longer settling for cheap "how to" sermons, personality cults, light and sound shows, anecdotal paranormal experiences, trite Bible study, or a half-inch deep spirituality.

Let us say it: the Protestant tradition has failed us. It has turned all of us into Narcissus. We steadily focus our gaze on ourselves, our voice, our journey, our experiences, our thoughts. We seek to relate God to ourselves. This navel gazing sickness is our inheritance as Protestants, and it is this that in a thousand forms is on sale in the Mall.

When we turn to the New Testament and the story of Jesus and the apostolic churches, one of the things we immediately see if we read it cover to cover is the paucity of recorded subjective experiences. Sure, the book of the Revelation is supposed to be one grand subjective experience; it is also code language. It is not a literal description of anything and those who turn to it as though it is miss the point of this highly political document couched in liturgical language. Outside of this "apocalyptic writing" (a type of discourse among marginalized Second Temple Jews), which by the way, has had an uneasy history with regard to its inclusion in the Bible (Luther and Zwingli both rejected it), outside of Revelation there are very, very few actual recorded "experiences" of the divine.

Jesus has one at his baptism, Paul has one on the road to Damascus, there are some "encounters" with angels in Acts—but other than that there is precious little.

The New Testament literature simply does not place a premium on people "sharing their experiences." It would seem that whatever it was that went on inside individuals was not nearly as important as something else. We humans do not need more or better or greater experiences.

WE NEED TO LEARN HOW TO INTERPRET THE MOMENT AS WELL AS THE PAST.

The desire to experience God is ancient. The question of how God is experienced, however, is answered in the New Testament with one very important term: discipleship.

Some of you just cringed because you bought a product called "Discipleship" in the Mall. You thought you were learning how to follow Jesus but it was a classic case of bait and switch. Instead of a leader they gave you an autocrat. Instead of friendship you found that you had purchased authoritarianism. Then you had to keep purchasing the upgrades with all the new rules.

Finally, at some point you tossed that item in the trash can. Well, good for you, because what they are selling is not anything like discipleship as Jesus teaches it.

Discipleship may have a mystical component, but it is not mystically focused. This is where our contemporary charismatic Christian friends have placed the cart before the horse. Inasmuch as the charismatic church is the fastest growing Christian movement globally it is important to address this false step they have made.

Let me give you an example, one of tens of thousands (and trust me there literally are tens of thousands of these kinds of zany examples).

There is a certain charismatic preacher who traveled the world holding meetings where he and his partner taught people how to "get drunk on the Holy Spirit." They talked about "toking the Ghost" and walked the streets with a little nativity figurine of the baby Jesus, offering people an opportunity to suck on the baby Jesus doll like a cigarette. Supposedly when they do so they will "get high on God."

I know. This is as stupid as it sounds, but these fellows have an avid following and their followers imitate them. Now imagine for a moment that you are someone who takes your faith seriously and you are walking down the street of your city when you are approached and invited to "toke on the baby Jesus."

You can stop laughing now.

Imagine the non-Christian walking down the street, whose knowledge of Christianity is minimal. What might they think of Christianity, Jesus, God, or the church after such an encounter?

You can stop crying now.

And I haven't even described the hilarity of the Jesus Is My Boyfriend store! Hunk Jesus, Surfer Jesus, blond Jesus with his Cary Grant chin and Leonardo DiCaprio eyes (sorry, Leo) . . . ooooh how he seduces us with his looooovvvveeee, we anticipate his penetration . . . .can you feel it yet, baby? It's weird, but customers writhe on the floor in this store while sampling products.

Whatever.

And they love pairing this Jesus with things bought in the God Bless America store. It makes for a rather gaudy mess. Rambo Jesus can be on your side!

My point is that those who promote the mystical as the be all and end all of the Christian faith, those who seek to make God into a drug, fulfill the dictum of Karl Marx that religion is an opiate.

Marx was right! Religion is a drug. It is designed to numb us from the hard realities of life. Its function is to remove us from this consciousness and place us in another where we actually think we are experiencing the divine, when all we are experiencing is ourselves as larger than life, as gods. Psychologists call this projection and Christianity is replete with it. It has created Jesus a hundred times over in its own image and likeness. It then gives you all manner of reason to actually avoid what Jesus teaches and models. It numbs you to his call and command. But you don't care because you have the bliss of the drug.

It is the drug that wants you to stop reading and put down this book.

Discipleship is the exact opposite of this. Jesus said if you want to be his disciple you must take up your cross. Taking up your cross and treating Jesus as a drug are worlds apart. The latter is all about feeling better, getting the brain to drip a few more drops of oxytocin and dopamine into the system. Carrying one's cross is about plumbing the depths of human relationships, allowing the pain and the reconciling to be real. Denying the painful realities of life is healthy neither psychologically nor spiritually.

I am not denying that there are mystical experiences that may bring bliss or fulfillment, overwhelming joy or ecstatic peace. I am saying that when they come they come as gifts. To create a method whereby a person constantly needs "injections" of the divine is to create a dysfunctional, crippled personality whose sole focus is their next injection. You may have met these types of people. Like an alcoholic or a drug addict, all they can do is talk about their "high" and focus on where and how they are going to get their next fix.

However, it is worse than you think. Some churches run programs that they call "Supernatural Schools of Ministry," where they claim to teach you how to "receive words from the Lord." Like the old-time Pentecostals who would have you come forward to be "baptized in the Holy Spirit" by having you rattle off some nonsensical syllables like "mama shabama malamdadi" until you were convinced you were speaking in tongues, these schools have perfected "methods" whereby a person can claim to have "utterances" from God.

It has been the sad experience of many that these utterances are often judgmental or manipulative or controlling.

Some schools claim that if you disagree with the leadership you are possessed by demons. They go further and claim that people who question the authority of the leader are filled with a "Jezebel spirit." Jezebel was the wife of Ahab, and in accounts in the Old Testament was not a very nice person who challenged the Israelite prophets (she did not have a happy ending). So it is when these leaders are challenged (often rightly) they can claim that the challenger has a "Jezebel spirit." This is just a form of manipulative exclusion where the leader is justified in not listening to alternative viewpoints that might upset their narrow-minded doctrinal apple cart.

Too many pastors and teachers in the church have a mind like cement: all mixed up and permanently set.

These types of ministries are personality driven and so become cult-like. In their desire to be accepted people will easily latch onto a person whose public persona is outgoing, brash, over the top, and controlling. Why? People want to be told what to think and how to behave. There is nothing more frightening for some folks than thinking for themselves. Or as Martin Luther King, Jr., has said, "Nothing pains some people more than having to think."

Genuine Christian mysticism does not deny the powerful impact of experience with the divine. Authentic Christian mysticism, however, is fused with cross-carrying discipleship. Real mysticism is not so much an upward journey as it is a downward journey, to the bottom of life, where sweat and blood and tears and pain, depression and anxiety reside.

Mysticism is not about grasping God. It is trusting that in the experiences of life where it *seems* like God is absent, God is doing God's best work. It is about trust.

What is trust? The apostolic word which is often translated into English as "faith" is *pistis*. The word *faith* has become too loaded with rotten baggage. The Greek term *pistis* is better translated as "trust." (There is a big book on this by Teresa Morgan, titled *Roman Faith and Christian Faith: Pistis and Fides in the Early Roman Empire and Early Churches*.) Followers of Jesus are "rectified by trust."

The capacity to trust is itself a gift, as Paul says. Why then don't we trust God?

We think we are trusting God when we are really just trusting in our theologies! So, when life crashes into our religious viewpoints and we can no longer believe what we used to believe we quit "having faith." This "quitting" is a work of the Spirit applying the cross of Jesus to our life and thinking. All we have ever known from the Mall of Consumer Christianity is "bad faith." This is not what Paul is talking about when you read your Bible and see the phrase "we are justified by faith" or "the righteous shall live by faith."

How then is our relationship with God made right? It is made right by God and we trust that this is so. We trust we are forgiven. It is *that* simple.

Whence our conundrum with *trust*, then?

In 1987, Philip Lee published *Against the Protestant Gnostics*. The thesis of this book has never been rebutted. It would be difficult to do so inasmuch as Lee presents reams of evidence within tightly packed and logically coherent arguments. Lee contends that American Protestantism, from its beginnings in colonial America, whether conservative Puritan or liberal Congregationalist, down to our own time, in the Christian Culture Wars, is sick with a disease. The disease is not new; it is quite ancient and is a virus that has affected Christianity from the beginning. One can already see its entrance in certain of Paul's opponents in Corinth and possibly Colossae. It can also be seen in the opponents who separated from the community behind the Fourth Gospel (commonly called the Gospel of John).

This disease is known as Christian Gnosticism. There are many things one could observe about this disease and its baneful effects on Christendom and church leaders from Paul to Irenaeus to Barth have contended against it. Gnosticism asserts that one is saved by knowledge, by *what* one knows and the emphasis on *how* one knows what one knows. Gnosticism is an approach to the Christian faith that is incompatible with it; it is akin to fitting a square peg in a round hole. It cannot be done, yet Christianity has been trying for 2,000 years to do just this!

Followers of Jesus are not saved by knowledge or certainty; they are redeemed because they trust in spite of what they think they can discern from their five senses. Listen again:

Knowledge cannot and does not save anyone. It matters little whether this knowledge comes from a pulpit or a university lecture hall. All knowing and knowledge done apart from the way God has revealed God's self in Jesus will only ever be false knowledge. If your "faith" is knowledge-based you would be better off building a home on the beach on an island in a hurricane zone. Your chances of surviving the storms of life would be greater than having a knowledge-based faith.

This is the point of connecting mysticism with cross-carrying discipleship. Faith is not about climbing mountains but about crossing deserts and dark valleys. Faith is a trusting that in spite of what we think we see, God sees quite differently. On the cross, where Jesus experienced the greatest agony of his life, the Bible says that God was doing something incredible: reconciling the world to God's self and thus reconciling us all to one another.

Mysticism is a downward descent to the divine. Mysticism seeks God is the midst of life, not in some otherworldly space.

Now I have critiqued the Charismatic excess to the consternation of some. Excess it is because it is Christian Religion on Steroids.

God is not a drug and the point of mysticism is not to make one feel better.

The point of genuine mystical encounter with God is to turn me to my neighbor.

In other words, real mysticism has a social implication. As long as one thinks that mystical experiences are to make one feel better, then once one has "taken the God drug," then one is satisfied.

This was never the case for Jesus. The Gospels record that Jesus spent a fair amount of time in the wilderness alone with God, whom he called "Abba" or "Daddy." The Gospels also record that he came back from these experiences and into the lives of the broken, the broken-hearted, the hopeless, the despairing, and the outcast, and brought them a message that they were included. He included them! When others in his culture excluded these marginalized lepers, prostitutes, and other assorted "sinners," Jesus announced that they were included. In other words, Jesus' mystical encounters with his Abba led him to walk into the lives of the socially broken and proclaim that as far as God was concerned they belonged.

It is true that part of his mission was to heal. I am not denying that aspect of Jesus' ministry. It is important to note that, as far as the Gospels are concerned, the miracles that Jesus did (and he couldn't always do them) were done *not* to alleviate pain and discomfort (which seems to be the point of modern charismania), but to re-socialize the outcast.

In Jesus' culture there were all kinds of reasons a person might be considered unfit for human society. When Jesus healed people he made it possible for them to be reintegrated into their families and their culture. I can't say I see this emphasis in so-called healing ministries. Instead these ministries have their own set of "holiness codes" whereby people who don't live up to the expectations and rules of the leader are outcast and damned. Only insiders are healed.

They have missed the point that Jesus healed outsiders. Or as he says, "I have come to seek and save the lost." Jesus came into people's "cross experiences," places where they had been marginalized, told they had been damned by God, and invited them into a vital, vibrant, and living relationship with God and with one another.

Jesus' mysticism has a politics; it is the politics of inclusion. You see, it includes *you*. His vision of God's reign was one that had no margins other than the margin of those who created a margin and placed themselves outside of God's circle because they could not bear to be with a God who included the luckless, the forlorn, the heretic, the questioner, the unclean, and the immoral. In other words . . . you.

I have taken some time guiding you around a number of the prominent stores in the Mall of Consumer Christianity in order to show you that the differences in their products are manifold but the materials and the toxins they use in their products are the same. The Jesus enthroned by the Father is *not* found in the Mall. You will search in vain for him. Until you realize that shopping there was a fruitless task in the first place.

Who is Jesus? Is he who we say he is? Is he the sum of our interpretations? Is he who scholars say he is? Or preachers, pastors, and Sunday school teachers? How can we even begin to hope that somehow, somewhere there is Truth.

You search for the Truth, but the truth is that the Truth has already found you!

CHAPTER 3

Crucifixion

The question of where we begin our thinking is one of the most important questions we can ask as we reflect on the character of God. Does it matter where we begin? Yes and no. "Huh?" you say. Let me explain.

In one sense you can only begin where you are. You may have some faith or no faith, strong faith or weak faith, intellectual faith or experiential faith, you may have blue faith or green faith or anti-faith, but all of us have a position in relation to that category called "god." So, where you are is where you must begin.

Christian faith does not begin at any of those starting points, those types of questions regarding faith are from Consumer Christianity, which is why many of you recognized various phases of your life having possessed various kinds of faith (dare I say "possessed by"?). The Christian Religion Shopping Mall (otherwise known as Protestantism) does not have a store or even a kiosk that sells the only starting point given to us in the gospel itself: the death of Jesus.

There are many things one can say with regard to Jesus of Nazareth's death and Consumer Christianity has found a way to make a fortune here, telling you Jesus was a sacrifice for your sins or that his death was just a political act or that it never really happened and all manner of assorted silliness. Worse is that the store that sells this stuff (Atonement Theory Unlimited) is one of the busiest!

Here is the problem: until you (yes, you) are offended by the twin assertions that Jesus is Lord (which in this case means affirming that he is deity) and that Jesus died, you have no idea what is really happening in Jesus' death. You will never get it as long as you are unwilling to call it "stupid," the stupidest thing you have ever heard. Who ever heard of a god dying? Gods do not die. Gods cannot really die. Gods swoop in and save the day. Gods are all-powerful.

Thing is, this kind of a superhero god makes no appearance at Calvary. In fact you can read all four Passion Narratives in Matthew, Mark, Luke, and John and nowhere does God appear. Nowhere. It is as if God is absent. Jesus is arrested, tortured, put on trial, condemned, executed, and dies. End of story. No God anywhere. That is the story the early Christians told. Why did they tell the tale that way?

At Calvary all god concepts die.

There is no Superman god at Calvary, there is no cavalry at Calvary, no holy host of angels to ride in and save the day, no Neo, no Luke Skywalker, no Jack Reacher. Nothing, nada, zip, zilch.

Jesus dies, end of story.

Why is it necessary for us to start with the death of all our god concepts? The Apostle Paul and the writer of the Gospel of John both tell us that it is impossible to understand God apart from Jesus' death, and to use Paul's words, label Jesus' death an absurdity. And an absurdity it is! It makes no sense at all, particularly if we have given up on the vampire god that demands Jesus' death as satisfaction for our sins. What could possibly be the point of Jesus' death if not to placate a god with an anger management problem?

So many of us grew up with this. A god that required sacrifice; a god that was a divine child abuser. Jesus took the hit for us, now God won't strike us with eternal punishment, AKA, hell.

Oh how we love Jesus. Yada, yada, yada.

But this is not the message of the New Testament.

Could it be, as Paul says, that we could not even begin to perceive what this might mean, no matter how hard we tried, if it were not revealed to us by God? The very fact that we might penetrate this absurdity only through the further absurdity of talking about God revealing God's self to us is truly absurd until we combine these two thoughts:

God died. We killed God.

We humans did it, and while we were doing that as supposedly civilized humans, God was doing something else. God was forgiving us. Luke records that while dying Jesus repeated over and over again "Father forgive them, they haven't a clue as to what they are doing." Paul says that in Jesus' death "God was reconciling the world to God's very self."

While you and I were killing God, God was forgiving us. Let that slam home in your brain.

Jesus' death is the end of all the gods sold in the Mall of Consumer Christianity. Unlike all the other gods who forgive at a cost, Jesus' does not. The Mall of Consumer Christianity despises the gospel because the gospel is *free* and if you can't make money off it why bother?

It exposes them all as idols, impotent at best, terrifying at worst. All the Protestant gods are fakes, fugazis, not worth the paper they are printed on. That is what Jesus' death does. It kills our ability to even talk about God from any intellectual, conceptual, religious, philosophical, or even psychological angle.

It is the end of everything we thought we knew about God, and because it is the end of our god concepts, Jesus' story alone creates space for an entirely new way of conceiving and knowing God.

If you are not blown away at this point, if something isn't stirring in your soul or eating away at your mind then . . .

Listen deeper.

The very thought that as you were killing God, Giver of your life, God was at the same time forgiving you, is the gospel. Paul remarks that the educated of his day found this stupid, the gods don't forgive, they get even and more! He also remarks that the religious of his day refused to see this because they could only conceive of God as a superhero and obviously no one came to save the day that Friday. The death of Jesus absolutely obliterates all of our understanding of who think God is or might be or could be. Jesus' death alone starts us at the right place.

Followers of Jesus affirm a crucified God.

In the 1960s *Time* magazine had the famous headline taken from the German philosopher Friedrich Nietzsche, "God is dead." The Christians of course did not like this and all manner of stores began opening in the Mall of Consumer Christianity seeking to disprove the death of God. The fact is Nietzsche was spot on, for he goes on to say, "God is dead and we have killed him." Yes, we, you and I, have killed God. So, since you and I live in the twenty-first century and we were obviously not there when Jesus died (unless you do some weird past life regression thing), how are you and I responsible for killing Jesus?

Last time I checked I was not a time traveler; I was not there 2,000 years ago when Jesus died, so how did I participate in killing Jesus?

The evidence lies in something we can see all around us.

Simple question: Have you ever been part of a group, church, or family system that turned on you and blamed you for its troubles? Ever feel like the black sheep, the odd one out, the one who didn't hear the music stop and failed to get a seat?

Now ask this question: have you ever been part of a group, church, or family that blamed someone else as the "real" problem? All of us have; we learned how to do this in children's games, we formed cliques in school, we became groups and communities as adults, and we all know how to find the "real" problem and get rid of them. And good riddance!

There is a term we use for this practice: *scapegoating*. I would venture to say that if you examine your life closely you can find many instances where a group of people has turned on you. I would also venture to say you can identify it when you see other groups scapegoating another and blaming them for their woes.

But I'll bet you could not identify many instances where you have engaged in such behavior. It is impossible for us to recognize our own complicity in scapegoating. The human mind cannot handle that it is unrighteously blaming a random person; it has to justify the blood on its own hands. We don't scapegoat; others may scapegoat but we don't. We are reasonable and rational. All of our expulsions are just and righteous.

The reality is that when a group experiences conflict and tension it seeks a focus for its internal dissonance until it finds the weakest and most vulnerable, the one who most are likely to join in blaming.

Then it points its finger, and you have a crucifixion, an assassination, a lynching, a murder, a life tossed out and thrown away BECAUSE THE GROUP IS CERTAIN IT IS A WORTHLESS LIFE.

All against one.

This is how we do this thing called humanity. We find our unity in the process of scapegoating. It is the scapegoat that brings our agreement to oneness; yes, we are all certain it was the fault of this person, she is to blame and here are the "reasons." The most amazing thing is that this process actually creates harmony and peace!

For awhile . . .

Then we get hungry again. Like zombies we have to have our flesh. The tensions within our family grow, or there are problems in our church, and bada boom, bada bing! The process starts all over again. It is a process that goes way back, long before Jesus. It is as old as Cain and Abel, Marduk and Tiamat, Romulus and Remus. Archaeologically we have evidence of this practice dating to circa 10,000 BCE at the Neolithic site Gobekli Tepe.

Human sacrifice.

We humans learned that the only thing that had the power to eliminate our social conflicts and the resulting violence was to apply a little homeopathic remedy: a little blood instead of a lot of blood. Sure, some would die, but the group would survive. In the beginning we would sacrifice the weakest among us: women, children, persons with visible deformities like a limp or blindness, and later prisoners of battle.

Who would want such people when they were clearly a burden? They wouldn't be the way they were unless the gods were displeased with them. Later we would justify this with myths. Now please understand that in our becoming human this does not take place consciously for tens or hundreds of thousands of years. It is just a process that works and it is non-conscious.

Until one day when someone consciously points a finger and the act of scapegoating is repeated where ritual (do what we did last time to get the desired results) and consciousness (this must be done and "I" take responsibility for doing it) are united and humanity ends up birthing religion and creating gods.

Sky gods, gods before whom we tremble, for they have to do with the ultimate reality: fear, and blood and death. Gods who punish transgression, gods who require blood whether in the frenzied ceremonies of the Aztecs or the more "rational" animal sacrifices of the Greeks, Romans, Jews, and Persians. Gods hate rule breakers. If a god is around, there will be blood; that is their operating system. All the gods get their operating system from the Apple (did you see what I did there?).

The death of Jesus is of this cosmic order: it has to do with the process that makes us civilized, able to do human relationships and human community. It strips away all our justifications for the process. Just as the Jewish high priest Caiaphas was sure he was righteously eliminating Jesus because it was "better that one man die than the nation perish," so we too, even to this very day, justify this behavior always in ourselves but never in others. We cannot see our own scapegoating practices. This is what the cross of Jesus reveals to us about ourselves.

We, you and I, have all participated and continue to participate, often unwittingly, in this dark and wicked practice, born in the snake pit of human imagination and reason.

This is our human crisis and it is ancient. No matter how civilized we become, no matter how scientifically brilliant we become, no matter how technologically advanced we become, all human cultures and groups still participate in this antique ritual *because we believe it has power*. It does have power, the power of death, and thus we stand in awe of it and we fear it. We fear the GOD behind it all without knowing that it is only ourselves that we fear. We have projected our sacrificial selves onto sacrificial gods because we could imagine no other kind of god than one that was like us.

Instead of the blindness of this projection, Jesus' death puts an end to it; he sheds light on it by exposing it: the alleged righteous act of a community is shown to be really unrighteous, indeed ungodly. Jesus was put to death on trumped-up charges. His own followers betrayed him, denied they knew him, and fled from him.

They followed the crowd who chanted his death sentence, "Lock him up, crucify him!"

Now Christians who shop in the Evangelical wing of the Mall read this story and feel sorry for Jesus.

Oh, poor Jesus, so abused for me and my sin. Poor Jesus, weep, weep.

This is a pathetic reading, for it first of all places God on the side of the persecutors (there is a justification for Jesus' death, namely to placate God's wrath). Second, it utterly fails to recognize that Jesus does not first invite us to join him in his victim status but to recognize we are the ones who drove the nails into his hands and feet, mocked him and tortured him. As the spiritual says, "Were you there when they crucified my Lord?"

When the answer becomes a resounding "yes" the tendency is to perceive one's self as an observer when the gospel invites us to see ourselves as the participants. We all did this and the proof in the pudding is that we still continue to do it. All against one. We know that mechanism works or at least we think we know and so we default to it every single time there is trouble in Doggyland.

The first essential step is to truly see yourself as one who joins the crowd, the mob, the group.

And while all of this is crucial to understanding Jesus' death, it has only really said what it is not.

There is another aspect of being an apprentice to Jesus that Consumer Christianity has failed to give you. It can't because if it offered the gospel to you, you would no longer purchase its products. The gospel offers you personally and all of humanity collectively a way out.

The gospel is about the way to live human life apart from scapegoating. The gospel creates an alternative way of being human and that alternative is borne witness to in the Gospels. Consumer Christianity has a totally false approach to Jesus' humanness. It approaches Jesus through its own lens and fails to see that it distorts the most important reality that he brings to the table.

Jesus means forgiveness.

Not through some divine transaction. Not because anyone deserves it. Only because he is doing the Father's will and that was all that mattered to him: to express forgiveness to us for murdering him and to start us on another path in light of that revelation of love, a path of reconciliation and peace.

The cross of Christ confronts us in the deepest most primal nonconscious part of being human. It deals with our originary bentness toward sacrificial religion, and brings it into the light so that it may turn to dust and blow away. Just as important, it also points the way we, following Jesus, may be those who truly imitate him, and thus imitate his Abba, as we learn to be the community that practices forgiveness with one another.

We are most like God when we forgive one another.

Admittedly this has not been put into practice much in 2,000 years, but it doesn't make it any less true with regard to a healthy vision of Christian relationships. Consumer Christianity has many ways of hiding the gospel light under the bushel of its Interpretations. If you meander through the history of Christianity you can easily see this done time and again and time and again the gospel breaks out. It is inevitable; the light shines in the darkness and the darkness is powerless to do anything but vanish.

Another way to express this is to say if at the cross all god concepts die then we might also note that the cross of Jesus is the beginning of what must be called Christian atheism. That is, followers of Jesus do not have a God like other gods. When you look at the way Consumer Christianity talks about its gods, have you noticed that they all have several things in common no matter how far apart they may be ideologically? All their gods must have recompense. Some call this God's holiness or righteousness, others God's justice, but whatever it is called it is always good for me and bad for you. Always.

God is always on my side, not yours. This is the commonality.

The reality is that God is not on either side; God is the victim strung up among them all, binding them all together with outstretched arms. And they cannot see it.

They are too busy cannibalistically consuming God to notice that it is God they are consuming. All their religious fantasies about an angry violent deity, a transcendence that meets just reward, clouds their minds as they madly chomp down those heavenly calories. All of this is clothed with transcendence, from stained glass and vaulted ceilings to seven-piece professional bands, lights, sound and fury. It is all one great big show of confirmation bias; the community is once again formed by who they are not, whom they despise and whom they would never in a million years be like.

The death of Jesus is God's "NO!" to this kind of human formation and relation. The cross is the BIG EVENT where we really got it all wrong and consequently get everything wrong. As such it forces us to acknowledge our propensities and tendencies to join the mob, the group, the crowd, sometimes out of anger, sometimes out of fear, just like Jesus' disciples did. Standing before the Christ of the cross we are all only asked one question and that is enough to start us on the path to new life: "Why do you persecute me?"

This is the question that brought Paul to his knees. This is the question that turned Paul from one who thought that killing the enemy was God's will to one who would, like God, become an intentional victim.

You are cringing. No one in their right mind would want to become a victim. For crying out loud, anyone who does that should have their head examined. We are going to explore this later and what it looks like and how it means.

In the meantime it sounds like this God and his followers are quite insane. I told you that if you bring the two phrases together, "While we were killing God, God was forgiving us" the implications would blow your mind. God died and while we were killing God, God was, in his beloved child Jesus, forgiving us.

God is not just any victim, God is the Forgiving Victim. God was never the angry retributive victim. Ever. God intentionally came right into the heart of all that makes us "human" and crashed the programming. Jesus put a divine virus in our faulty programming, our seduction, our illusions, our lies, and our grievous sin, as a species, when he became the One in the All against One mechanism. He cracked religion at its core with his story. In their song "Hymn," Barclay James Harvest sings:

> He told great stories of the Lord
>
> He said He was the Savior of us all
>
> For this we killed and nailed him on high
>
> He rose again as if to ask us "Why?"

Why indeed? Why?

But we would know none of this if not for something else. Without that something else, Jesus' death would have faded into history of one of the many thousands of crucifixions that took place in the centuries before he lived and afterward.

We know nothing apart from this Something. It can be put this way:

Who is it that is asking you, "Why do you persecute me?"

CHAPTER 4

Resurrection

There is a cultural fascination with death, one could say an obsession with death, in our world today. Horror as a literary, cinematic, and kinesthetic art form is big business. We have created all manner of terror from medieval depictions of hell and Satan to ghosts, zombies, and other living dead. From Mary Shelley's *Frankenstein* to Steven King's *It*, we have created all manner of terrors and horrors associated with death.

We fear death more than anything. In our world, death is the last experience. Death turns a living being into a memory . . . just . . . like . . . that. When I was a hospital chaplain I had many experiences of being with people when they died, and with one exception that I can recall, there was always a very palpable fear of death. Family members in waiting rooms with their grief, fears, and emotional distress were a chorus of lamenting witnesses to the power of death.

A thief had come in the night and stolen our most precious treasure.

We fear death because death has power over us. It is this fear that constitutes death's power. We give anything power over us when we fear it. Death has become the human master. Even though "dying" is built into the universe (if you are honest in your physics), we are the species that brought death. We created *it* in the beginning. We were Cain slaying Abel. We were the group, the crowd, the mob that took all of our collective hostilities out on one that was different. We *murdered* and we called it *good*!

Ever since death has hovered over us like a long dark shadow because down deep within us is always a squirming question, a doubt, perhaps even a fear that we have violated something ancient, some rule built into the universe. And just as we unrighteously judged our scapegoat, so we inject judgment into death and create all manner of religious scenarios where no matter how it all ends, we are the ones on the right side of judgment while all others perish. We *lie* to ourselves about all of this. All of our religion and all of our cultures are grounded in and built on a great big LIE, the LIE that any one life is expendable as long as the group survives.

It was this LIE that Jesus brought light to, it was this lie that he crushed, every argument. Every authority, every footnote this argument could bring was utterly crushed when he changed all our understanding of what it means to persecute and what it means to be a victim as he died.

"Father, forgive them, they haven't a clue as to what they are doing." Then Jesus expired. He was buried. And that was that.

But . . .

Maybe "the end" is not really The End.

The disciples lived in absolute fear for several days after Jesus' death. They knew how they acted, they knew what they said and what they did . . . and what Judas did. They had actually believed that Jesus fit all their conceptions of Messiah, and now all that was dashed, and worse was that a) the authorities could be seeking them so as to root out tree and branch and b) God was surely angry and somehow, someway, this did not bode well for anybody, especially them.

Suddenly in the midst stands the Victim, who says two things:

"Peace" and "Do not fear."

If we have listened to the question of persecution honestly in our deepest self, then this is the answer that we hear.

Peace, wholeness, restoration, *life* itself.

And a peace where there is no fear, for this peace is pure love and perfect love casts out all fear. This is a message of reconciliation.

Why these words?

The disciples upon seeing Jesus in their midst before he speaks could have only be said to have made a deposit in their pants. This was pure terror! The One they had forsaken, denied, and betrayed was in the their midst and the only thing they could think of was recompense and judgment. This entire way of thinking is dispelled with these words:

"Peace."

"Do not be afraid."

All is well. There is nothing that is not well. ALL is WELL! Julian of Norwich was right.

The sheer incomprehensibility of this and a demonstration that this extraordinary insight needs time to seep into our souls can be found in the opening chapter of the biblical book of Acts. The disciples have been with the risen Jesus for forty days and presumably he is teaching them and still, just before he leaves the material plane, they are stuck in their theology, waiting for Jesus to bring the Day of Judgment and Recompense ("Lord, when will you restore the kingdom to Israel?"). I have to think that a certain kind of wry smile crossed Jesus' face at that point and a divine sigh was expelled. But it was a loving smile nonetheless.

This is very difficult inasmuch as the entirety of the Mall of Consumer Christianity only sells gods of Judgment and Recompense. The risen Jesus shows us the character of the One he calls "Abba" and from the perspective of the gospel judgment and recompense are not the solution but the problem. It is this problem of our poor theology, our bloodthirsty gods, and our imitation of them in our lives that is addressed in Jesus' life, death, and resurrection.

But there is another point to observe. There is no single resurrection appearance story in the New Testament where the risen Jesus is immediately recognized. The disciples in the upper room suppose they have seen a ghost, the two disciples walking with Jesus for hours have no idea who he is, Mary of Magdala supposes Jesus to be a cemetery gardener, and finally, Paul's great question could well have been asked by them all:,

"Who are you . . . God?"

Simply put, we do not recognize the risen Jesus when he "appears" to us. We can't. He has to reveal himself to us as the victim: "I am Jesus whom you are persecuting." Or he calls our name: "Miriam." Or he begins an internal dialogue but we have no idea it is Jesus conversing with us until we sit down to give thanks and eat. Then in each case

Bam!

It hits us like a ton of bricks . . .

Whenever we persecute another we are really persecuting Jesus, indeed God, in them. We are guilty of theocide every time we justify excluding, extruding, ostracizing, and ultimately killing. And for all of our lifetime's worth of hurting others and dealing death to

God through others (thinking we were bringing death from God), we hear the word:

You are forgiven.

No ifs, ands, or buts.

Just straight up, no rocks, no chaser.

When the light of divine forgiveness penetrated the darkness and fear of death, it took sin with it, and sin passed away into that which amounts to nothing. This is why, as James Alison says, "we only know sin as it is being forgiven."

Sight comes only through Easter eyes.

For those of you that are still thinking in terms of sin as the breaking of laws and commandments, or as personal peccadillos, you are missing the point of Jesus' death. Those are just symptoms of the Sin that gives rise to all sin: the principle of retribution.

It is our human "nature" to create scapegoats, to affirm our identity as "not that," and to require those who dishonor or disrespect us and our religion be brought to justice. Jesus' death exposes all this as a Lie and the resurrection affirms and validates not only that but also the only way of being human that is truly divine.

We broke his body and he offered us his blood, a blood that did not cry from the earth for retribution and judgment but, unlike the blood of Abel, Jesus' blood cried out for mercy and forgiveness. He was uttering the Abba's words for he only did what the Abba did and said what the Abba said. He imitated his Abba to the max and he said so.

Jesus resisted the temptation to violence in Gethsemane when he could have called legions of angels to come and start a holy war and save him. He went the way of the long road to the cross where he did not utter recriminations or call for justice, but from his heart sought mercy, compassion, and forgiveness to those who perceived him as the problem, as the enemy.

For this reason, the Abba was pleased to grant him Life in himself, and completely and totally vindicated Jesus' decision as well as his life's message and ministry in bringing him to life. But again, not life that is recognized by us. It is life that cannot be categorized with our rational structures, our conceptions of history, our ideational philosophies or our religious traditions for it is Life outside of our complete and total understanding of what constitutes life. It is a *totally other* kind of life, and so it takes time for us to see and to understand and to comprehend. It takes *time*. It does not come all at once. The insights that Life brings are so earth shattering to our whole and total existence and the way we do this thing called human are reoriented so that our journey with the risen Jesus often feels like walls just keep coming down. And they do!

And that is *good*!

Just as our intellectual and religious traditions cannot handle the scandal of the cross, so they fall utterly into syllabic nonsense when it comes to the presence of the Living Jesus. Inside the Mall of Consumer Christianity one can find all manner of merch relating to the story of Jesus' resurrection appearances. Some of the products offer manifold (ir)rational explanations (the Apologetics Plus store), others deny the risen Jesus altogether, fabricating all manner of speculation (the Philosopher's Stone store).

As long as we come to the risen Jesus expecting the same kitsch that we bought in the Mall, he will only ever be as a stranger to us. The fact is the Risen Jesus explodes and dismisses all of our theological, religious, and intellectual ways of thinking. Why? The same mechanism that produced religion also produced culture and with it philosophy. Intellectual sacrifice is the same as social sacrifice. The gospel intrudes on all of that as an alien virus. Encountering the gospel of the risen Jesus is to have one's entire view of all transfigured and transformed, and this is absolutely done right where it must start:

The risen Jesus *is* the crucified Jesus with one congruent message of forgiveness, peace, and the Answer to the Great Riddle of life.

What exactly is at the heart of all of this?

Jesus is the singular point by which and from which we must talk about God. He is the Forgiving Victim whose only mission and purpose is to reconcile all creation back to his Abba by revealing God to be the self-revealing merciful and beneficent One.

Jesus is the mirror image of the Abba, a chip off the old block; like father, like son.

This is huge for a real problem of the Christian tradition. The (un)-natural tendency in Christian theology has been a create a split between "God" and Jesus. Consumer Christianity offers a good cop/bad cop god relation between "God" and Jesus. The stalls and kiosks of the Mall all have variations on this but in the end there is always some kind of judgment, recompense, justice, or punishment coming to us from this "God."

This is not the Abba, the Creator of all things. No, these are all the gods of our human nightmares created by us when we deemed evil as good in our primal beginnings. The Abba forgives, the Abba does not judge. Jesus forgives, Jesus does not judge. And finally the Spirit of the Abba sent to us through Jesus so we can recognize her does not judge but is our advocate, our guide, and our teacher.

This is more popularly known as the doctrine of the Trinity. The fact is even though Christianity has said it believes in one God, it actually has two gods, for Jesus is not like "the Father." Christians have found clever ways of distributing their yin and yang, mercy and justice, heaven and hell between the so-called members of the Trinity. In so doing they turn the Abba of Jesus into one of the bloodthirsty judgmental gods of human religion. In this sense there is very little difference between the god of the Aztecs and the god found in the Mall.

An authentic beginning for thinking about the character of God must begin with the words of Jesus from the cross, and the resurrection appearances. These words describe the New Reality of Light and Life and they simply do not fit any of the ways we have customarily learned to think about things. Within all our human rationality we only know one thing: Death.

Why would the Abba raise Jesus from the dead? Because Jesus took with him into death itself the only reality that could overcome death.

Forgiveness.

Forgiveness is the invincible reality manifested in Jesus. Forgiveness conquers all. Love is forgiveness. Love restores by forgiving, love heals through forgiving. Forgiveness is the Light that is the only beginning point for our individual and species healing.

Nothing can vanquish forgiveness, for forgiveness' presence turns all that is tainted by sin and death to vapor, as light banishes darkness. Now do you understand how Jesus could have such confidence that since he did the Father's will, that the Father would not allow Death to have the final word?

When Jesus brought forgiveness into Death and the grave he brought that which death could not handle. Forgiveness ate away at the core of death and rendered it powerless because we had always assumed death meant judgment, because death has to do with sin. Forgiveness vaporized Death by taking away its illusory power of fear.

This willingness of God to forgive our most heinous sin, our human "doing," our bentness toward death, ruined death forever. The risen Jesus comes to us as a stranger but if we listen and follow him, and as we get to know his voice through the Spirit, we find that death has no power over us for the fear of death has no power over us.

As he faced his doom in Gethsemane, how did Jesus find the confidence that no matter what happened to him his Abba would not have his death be the end of his story?

For the previous years of his public ministry, his teaching and acts were suffused with forgiveness. Jesus trusted that he had authority to forgive the sins of others and wipe their slates clean. Jesus trusted that the One at work in him was an Abba who loved and cared for people as a mother dotes on her children.

Jesus trusted his Abba, plain and simple. Jesus knew his Abba, the one he, as a human, would refer to obliquely as God, loved him. Jesus knew this without a doubt and says as much in various ways throughout the Gospels. Jesus had confidence that his Abba loved him so completely that not even death could permanently sever that bond. Jesus may have indeed feared being killed—according to some texts of Luke he sweat drops of blood—but he did not fear death.

Jesus died doing his Abba's will expressing the heart of God as One Who Forgives. He took that forgiveness to all theologies of hell and judgment and recompense, and death, and shone such a brilliant light with such an intense otherworldly energy that all of this, all darkness, all fear, was sucked into it and obliterated.

The death of Jesus is the divine black hole that sucks all that is evil in and exhales life, light, and love.

In Jesus' death we are all found as forgiven persecutors. In his resurrection we are renamed as his brothers and sisters. That, my friend, is the gospel.

In light of all this how can we then talk about the presence of God in our lives so that it is authentic to the gospel itself?

CHAPTER 5

Ascension

If you are starting at this chapter you will have made a grievous error. You will soon find yourself confused or at odds with everything being said here. This is not the starting point. The proper starting point is in chapter 3, so go back and begin there or what follows will be of little benefit to you.

The big Christian holidays are Christmas and Easter. Both are money-making events for the Mall. It is true that both have significant theological and liturgical implications for the Christian life and time (the Christian liturgical year). We are quite familiar with these stories, especially if we are "go to church twice a year" folk!

However, as the story of Jesus is told in the early church, there is almost no emphasis on the Christmas story; Mark, John, Paul, and the writer of Hebrews place no emphasis there. The Easter story has more annual significance than Christmas in the early church but even there the emphasis, as we will saw in the previous chapter, is on the resurrection of the crucified Jesus. The resurrection is not a thing in itself but is intimately connected to the Passion narrative.

For the earliest Christians there was another event that made all of this meaningful and powerful in their lives: their confession that the Creator of all things had affirmed, vindicated, and valorized the life of the man from Nazareth. According to Paul, this valorization was so complete that "God" gave to Jesus, the Jew from Nazareth, God's own name, the Tetragrammaton (YHWH), the Unpronounceable Name, or as the Jewish tradition put it:

Ha Shem, the Name.

Jesus was given the Name. The Abba recognized Jesus as the faithful Son. This event, which scholars call Jesus' Session at the Right Hand of Majesty, is celebrated in May as the Day of Ascension and this day is pretty much passed over by the Mall. Not a whole lot of Happy Ascension Day greeting cards to be found there.

Seriously, have you ever purchased one?

Yet if I asked you to name the one text from the Jewish Bible (or what the Mall calls the Old Testament) that is quoted more times in the apostolic writings than any other do you think you could tell me what it is?

It is Psalm 110:1: "The Lord said to my lord, 'Sit at my right hand until I make your enemies a footstool for your feet.'"

Who is it that sits at the right hand of majesty? Is it not one "like a lamb slain"? Is it not the crucified and risen Jesus? As the writer of the sermon "To the Hebrews" says, it ain't exactly a great and powerful angel that sits there. Nor, would I add, is it a mythical or Marvel superhero. He who sits at the right hand of the Abba, who has been given the Name and who thus has all authority over all things, is a human being just like you and me. Look again—it is no Superman or Wonder Woman who sits there. The One who sits there has scars. That One went through hell and back. That One who was sent and came unto his own and was rejected by them and who continues to be rejected by Consumer Christianity because he does not fit their itsy bitsy teeny weeny nano-theologies.

Who is it whom God recognizes? Jesus of Nazareth. This means that everything about him, his life, and his teaching have been given divine authorization. And like so many other places this is where Consumer Christianity gets it all wrong. They have turned the ascended Christ into their own personal magic wand who is a Great Big Superintendent of Buildings in the Sky. Got a problem? Make a call and the Super will come and fix it.

Consumer Christianity, because it has not started at the cross, turns Jesus into another Sky God. Heracles, Rambo, John D. Rockefeller. Sky gods come in more than 5,000 flavors! The many Jesuses of Consumer Christianity all have this in common: God is all-powerful and power is conceived of as the power to judge and kill. Herein lies another toxin at the heart of Consumer Christianity.

Power is misconceived. Human religion and culture can only think of power in a dualistic framework: power is always power over another. Parents have power over their children. In many cultures, including certain Christian cultures, men have power over women. The state has power over all its citizens. The church has power over all her members. Pastors or elders have power over their congregations. Whites have power over blacks, and rich have power over poor.

Whether one speaks of culture or religion, *power* is all about might, strength, the ability to crush, coerce, force, compel.

Funny thing is that when we examine carefully the life and teaching of Jesus we do not seem to find this understanding of power. We do see a different power at work, and we admire it and wish for it, maybe even hope for it. But we do not see that power much in our lives or churches or world. We mostly see power over and thus think of God's power this way. This is just another religious illusion dispelled by Jesus' death and we are ill-advised to set such an illusion up at the right hand of God, yet that is exactly what Christians have done. Rather than say with the historical crowds that Jesus possessed an unusual authority (in other words, that he comes to them as a "stranger"), Christians have found all manner of ways to turn Jesus into their own image rather than allowing his story to describe theirs.

It is important that you understand that much of the apostolic writings (the New Testament) concern false views of Jesus. The little letter of 1 John ends with the admonition to "stay away from idols", idols which have been defined in the letter as poor portraits of Jesus. This was huge for the apostolic churches, for they understood the intimate and crucial reality of describing and defining deity only in terms of Jesus.

You become the god you worship; you live the god you worship.

Consumer Christianity has put ingredients in its products that are harmful and have been shown to cause spiritual and intellectual cancer of the eyes in humans. Humans have, from long consumption, become blind to the Living Lord (in theological language the *Christus Praesens*). It really does not matter whether you are a conservative Evangelical or a Liberal, a Fundamentalist or a Progressive Christian; the same Jesus is found in all your stores. At some point you have introduced the justification of violence or "power over" into the story of Jesus and thus into the story of God, and you have drunk the Kool-Aid. One ought not only think of the maniac Rambo Jesus from the sky of Fundamentalists; Liberal calls for social justice use threats of "power over" just as their twins, the Fundamentalists, do; the revolutionary SJW Jesus is ever present here.

But these Jesuses are fake precisely because they have failed to make the announcement that Jesus proclaims: God is forgiving, God is not retributive.

Jesus sought forgiveness on the cross. He took forgiveness into hell and wiped it off the map. Therefore, God called that life

Life and gave Jesus New Life. In the same manner Jesus carries forgiveness back to its starting point when he "ascends" to the Father. The Jesus seated at the right hand of the Father has seated forgiveness with him.

Forgiveness is enthroned!!

This is not so in either Liberal or Conservative Mall stores. The forgiveness of the gospel is denied in the one tradition (where there is no sin there is no need for forgiveness) and turned into common religion in the other (it comes with a generic angry god). The entire Mall of Consumer Christianity has placed an idol at the right hand of God. Is it any wonder that so few enlightened persons see this? Customers cannot see what the Consumer Christianity has done to Jesus. I mean, how different is Tim LaHaye and Jerry Jenkins's *Left Behind* Jesus from Reza Aslan's *Zealot* Jesus. Not much, not much at all. But the Mall has convinced shoppers they are different when they are identical! Ergo, more sales!

False Advertising!

The non-retributive Christian life is just as discontinuous with the world as Jesus was from his religion. However, Consumer Christianity is nothing other than justification for the sacrificial ways of the world. Just as many of Jesus' contemporaries conceived of God within categories of justice, righteousness, anger, wrath, holiness, even if all of these were allegedly tempered with love, mercy, compassion, etc., so too the Protestant Mall offers such two-faced deities in every store. Oh, the sales people tell you "it's in the Bible" or "God's attributes must be held in tension" or "No one wants a namby pamby god," but really all they are trying to do is to get you to get your fix with them.

Divine forgiveness of *all* sticks in the windpipes of Consumer Christianity. They can't swallow it, it causes them to choke.

In stark contrast to Consumer Christianity, Paul, the writer of the Gospel of John, Luke, the writers of Mark and Luke-Acts, and the writer "To the Hebrews" share one very important understanding: any description of the character of God was only valid in terms of Jesus of Nazareth, the Jesus who resisted the worldly view of power in the temptation narratives, who again resisted it after the feeding of the 5,000, and who resisted it yet a final time in Gethsemane. It is Jesus' refusal to understand power as "power over," his absolute and clear rejection of any use of force in relationships, his rebuttal to those who understood power this way that paved the way to the cross and at the same was our salvation.

A human who bears scars, but one whose scars testify to forgiveness and reconciliation, is who sits at the right hand of God. Just as Jesus did not condemn persons during his lifetime, so he does not condemn them when he sits at the Abba's right hand. To say that during his lifetime Jesus came showing grace but that the flip side of the coin, namely judgment and recompense, are coming after death, is just another way of creating a good cop/bad cop scenario, only this time one has not done it in the Father-Son relationship, now it is done as a temporal sequence with Jesus' story. Christians do this only because they only know how to read the Bible through the lens of the bloodthirsty gods of religion. The way Consumer Christianity read its Bible is no different than the way early hominids interpreted rituals of human sacrifice. Some things never change.

Another false move made in Consumer Christianity is to either deny Jesus' humanness or his Godlikeness. Many stores in the Mall wanting to sell you a superhero Jesus claim he is just like you except you sinned and deserve punishment; Jesus did not sin and obeyed God's laws and that is why God accepted him. Jesus is mostly like you but not completely like you.

Paul would say "*Skubala*" to this. Excrement, poo poo, doo doo, kaka. I refrain from other colloquialisms but you are thinking of them!

God did not accept Jesus for what he did any more than you accept your children for what they do. You love them no matter what they do because they are your children (unless of course, you are dysfunctional). If you love your children in spite of their mistakes and rebellion and the pain they cause you, how much more can we say that a Father of Love loved the Son just because they are in that kind of familial relationship?

The Son who sits at the right hand is just like you and me. The apostolic writers had many ways of saying this: "The Logos became flesh" (Gospel of John), "Jesus took on sinful flesh" (Paul), "Jesus was made just like you and me" (Hebrews). They all affirm that Jesus is the Son of the Abba and that he willingly chose to be sent in order to become like us *in every way*, so that in every way we would be healed and restored. As one early church figure said, "That which is not assumed cannot be healed." It is important to know that the Jesus who sits at the right hand of God knows what it is to live a divine existence in the midst of human culture and religion, because that is where we live when we follow him.

Other stores like the "Jesus Is a Social Justice Warrior" store have denied that Jesus was sent by the Father, filled with the Father's Spirit, and raised from the grave by the Father. He did nothing "miraculous" in his lifetime and everything that cannot be explained in so-called scientific language is relegated to the Fantasy and Legend kiosk. This Jesus has a string that when pulled utters various politically correct, innocuous sounding but noxious sayings (like "no justice, no peace") that when put together form a Jesus that bears a strange resemblance to John Carpenter's *The Thing*; somehow human but utterly bizarre.

If we are willing to forsake the idols of Consumer Christianity and turn to Jesus of Nazareth as proclaimed by the apostolic tradition, we do not find a lofty figure, a CEO that doesn't know middle management let alone the woman in the mail room. Nor do we find a lawgiver with a zillion expectations that we seem to find and more creative ways of disappointing. Nor do we come to judge who hands out fines and punishments. Nor do we come to One who affirms identity politics and our definition of what constitutes justice. Jesus is no more a friend of Evangelical legalism than he is of progressive Christian liberation theology. His humanness transcends these categories, and names them all as sacrificial, as theology done by Cain, the human who went wrong and brought Death, and created religion and civilization.

When we come to Jesus we come to a human person, but more than that, we come to the True Human, the One whose humanity was properly done, so to speak. We come to One who knows our weaknesses, who was tested in all manner of ways just as we are, and who, by listening to the Abba, became truly and fully human. It is not our humanness that saves us; it is Jesus' humanity and the gift of that humanity to us that saves us.

How does this happen?

It is at this point that we see the apostolic church struggling to find a way to articulate this, but they all refer to Jesus' presence with us as the Spirit or the Holy Spirit. Now before you go thinking of spooks and things that go bump in the dark, this is not that.

The apostolic church did not have a thought-out view of the Holy Spirit. For the first four centuries the churches battled over the Father-Son relationship and the Holy Spirit gets a bare mention in the creeds. Nothing is fleshed out. Point of fact is that a gospel understanding of the Holy Spirit has yet to be written.

When we examine the apostolic writings there are several important themes associated with the Spirit. The first thing we observe is that there are various ways to refer to the Spirit: the Spirit of God, the Holy Spirit, the Spirit, the Spirit of Jesus. The best parts of the early church did not think Jesus was somewhere out there in Happy Clappy Sky God Land, they trusted that he was with them in their worship and in their discipleship. They trusted that it was Jesus with them, manifested now in the Spirit rather than the flesh.

But it was the same Jesus!

A second observation relates to the work of the Spirit. Paul speaks of the Spirit praying deep within us, for us, when we do not know how or what to pray. The writer of Hebrews insists it is Jesus that is our mediator (our priest) before the Abba. Is it the Spirit that prays for us or Jesus? Why get all confused?

Just as Jesus emptied himself and by imitating the Abba allowed the Father to stamp Jesus with the divine image, so also the Spirit empties herself and allows herself to be stamped with Jesus' image. This divine self-emptying is not limited to just Jesus; divine self-emptying is the divine mode of being. This is how the early church was able to confess that Jesus was present with them and also "discriminate" between Jesus and the Spirit.

A third observation has already been mentioned, namely the mediatorial work of the Spirit. The Spirit mediates Jesus to us just as Jesus mediates the Abba to us and thus the Spirit mediates the Father to us. She owns the Child just as the Child owns the Father for she is the Spirit sent from the Father through the Son. We can also say that just as Jesus mediates the Father to us, so as the Spirit bears his image, he also mediates the Spirit to us. Once again we find it impossible to even speak of "God" apart from this language of Father, Child, Spirit.

The presence of the Spirit *is* the presence of the One God, the One who is Love and Light and in whom there is no dark side, no shadow of turning, no anger management problem. Now just to show you how much you still need to purge the narcissism of Christianity from your veins, is it not the case that you have a question tumbling down the lane of your mind:

"Ok, Michael," you say. "If God is with me how come it doesn't feel like God is with me?"

Notice where the starting point of that question lies: it begins with you and your feelings. That is just the drug of religion trying to find a reason for you to go the Mall and get your fix. What you seek is a Sky God, a superhero, a little numbness to your current situation. Why do you do this?

You want a fix-it god because you have identified your circumstances with the favor or disfavor of God. When you bought products called Grace and Love and Forgiveness and such at the Mall, you were given instructions to operate them. These instructions all told you that in order for the product to work right there were things you needed to do and there were things that were prohibited.

You look at your life and if circumstances are in your favor, you must be blessed by God; but when things go poorly and life starts to fall apart all the old voices and tapes of culture and religion start playing in your head and you can only assume you violated some part of the fine print and have found divine disfavor. There is a technical term for this:

Deuteronomic hermeneutic.

Don't try to say this fast or you will twist your tongue.

Deuteronomic refers to the book of Deuteronomy in the Jewish Scriptures and hermeneutic means "interpretation." In this case the Deuteronomic hermeneutic expresses the view of that author that life consists of blessings and curses and if rules are obeyed and the rule of law respected, all will be well with your soul, but if you transgress the rules, God will make your life a living hell.

How nice. How utterly arcane.

Jesus tore that thinking to shreds when he said that God makes rain to fall on both good and evil and sun to shine on just and unjust. God does not discriminate good people from bad people the way we do. God loves the whole world, no exceptions. The early Christians were so bold as to sing in their worship that God had reconciled *all things* in Jesus (see the hymn in Colossians 1:15–20).

Circumstances are never a barometer of the Abba's love. For all apparent purposes the historical Jesus was a loser. Yet he knew that he was deeply loved by the Creator and nothing could sunder that love. He preached it, he shared it, he lived it, he taught it. He died demonstrating it, he was raised vindicating it, and that Love was enthroned when Jesus sat down at the right hand of the Abba.

Circumstances are just that: circumstances. They are not a measure of anything when it comes to God. This is what the Spirit of Jesus has been seeking to teach Christians since she was first sent. However, religion intruded, some early Christians could not fathom such a love and set in motion that which would eventually become the Christian Religion. For 2,000 years the Spirit of Jesus has been calling to her followers to be free from this kind of thinking and to be set free to trust the Father.

So, the Spirit sent from the Abba through the Son is she who brings us to birth at the cross and who brings us life through the resurrection and who brings confidence through the enthronement of Jesus. She is a wonderful counselor, a heavenly advocate, counselor or defense attorney who stands by us and with us when like Jesus we become the scapegoat of our families, groups, churches, and cultures. She is the One who takes away our fears, calms our souls, and speaks to us, so that our speech and actions at these times can be Jesus-like and thus moments of divine revelation for the mob.

She reminds us ever, only, and always of Jesus, nothing else.

She shows us how to live in trust as a fish swims in water. She shows us and empowers us to listen to Jesus and as we heed his words, we become like him. Our humanity becomes transformed! We cease to be nonconscious agents of sacrifice and become vessels of the love of God.

Through the Spirit we recognize with Paul that even though life itself is pressing hard upon us, we are not crushed. We know that even though all appears hopeless and lost, it isn't, for Death has been conquered. We sense that even though life appears as a chaos, overwhelming us at times, there is an underlying "meaning" to all of life, all of our personal stories. Yes, this too is given by the Spirit.

In his most extended discussion of the Spirit (in the Letter to the Romans chapter 8), the Apostle Paul is clear that "neither death nor life, nor angels, nor principalities, nor powers, nor things present, nor things to come, nor life, nor death *nor any other thing* shall be able to separate us from the love of God in Jesus." Nothing can separate us from this love, not even the ranting and raving preachers and teachers and other lunatics that stand outside the Mall and hawk their wares. No, we are held in the very heart of the Father in Jesus.

Here is the beauty of all this: While we may no longer believe or accept a Sky God that swoops in to save the day, we do affirm that God is behind the scenes of our life weaving a tapestry for good, or as Paul says "God works all things together for good for those who love him, for those called according to God's purpose."

Whoa! Hold on a minute, there are two qualifiers to this really good news. The first is "those who love him," the second is "those called according to his purpose." First, we need to ask what this business of loving God looks like.

Consumer Christianity only sells products where "Christian love" is obedience to rules or worldviews. Go to the stores and what do you find: Every group has its own special rules you must obey if you "love God." This is *not* the gospel; it is just another form of religion, as we have seen.

We love God when we trust God. We love God when we affirm the message we have given to be truthful and full of grace.

As we trust this redemptive message, as we learn not to use life circumstances as a barometer of the love of God for us, as we trust that we are forgiven, as we trust that Jesus is present with us by the Spirit, so we trust that whatever life hands to us, the Father is weaving a tapestry, weaving Jesus into the very fabric of our humanity like gold filigree.

We trust that what we think must be an ugly garment for all manner of social, philosophical, moral, ecclesial, psychological, and intellectual reasons is actually going to turn out quite beautiful because we know that we love God and have been called according to a purpose.

Now I am *not* speaking of the imaginary Calvinist "purpose" of Rick Warren's *The Purpose Driven Life*. Our purpose is not obedience to a sacrificial god, as Warren supposes. Our obedience reflects that of Jesus who surrendered all his rights and refused all manner of retribution and who listened to the voice of his Abba and reflected in his life and teaching the character of the Abba. In the chapter on crucifixion we called this "discipleship" and allowed the narrative arc of Jesus' story to fill in what this looked like. The purpose of God is to flesh out our humanity with Jesus' humanity, a humanity evidenced in the Gospel stories.

The Spirit does not play games with us; every moment, every thought, every word, every action, every emotion, every insight, every conversation, every event no matter how ill or ill-conceived is bent toward "the good." This may be our own good or it may be the good in general, but either way nothing is lost.

Circumstances are what they are and how we engage and respond to them indicates whether we have been eating spiritual junk food from the Food Court or are truly consuming heavenly bread. Just as there is an obesity crisis in America today so there is a dire spiritual obesity crisis in Christianity. Consumer Christianity has become so huge it can no longer get out of its chair and it is in mortal danger of a heart attack or spiritual cancer from all the toxins it has ingested.

Again, this is why we must begin at the cross and there recognize with Paul that what seemed like a horrible and tragic ending, a story with no God present, was actually the story that would save creation itself. This is why we can only make sense of the resurrection of Jesus, his enthronement and the sending of the Spirit in light of the cross and the character of God revealed in Jesus' dying. We keep circling back round and round again to the cross even when discussing Jesus our priestly mediator and the mediating work of the Spirit. Our understanding of all things, including the risen and authorized Jesus, takes its starting point from the cross.

This is how we trust that indeed as we listen to the voice of the Spirit of Jesus, we are transformed by the same Spirit into the image and likeness of Jesus, the very same Jesus who was crucified, raised from the grave, and seated at the right hand of the Father—Jesus, the same yesterday, today, and forever.

What might this look like in our human reality?

CHAPTER 6

Incarnation

How do we become like Jesus? What was his spiritual journey like? If we could know his spiritual journey, surely we could copy that and thus become "divine" (as in the Orthodox sense of "'divinization'" [*theosis*], a term becoming more familiar to the West)

However, at this very point we have an insurmountable problem.

Jesus had a spiritual journey but we know almost nothing about it!

The Gospels only give us the glances of a glimmer into his spiritual life; they record almost none of his prayers (Matthew 11:25–27 is an exception, as is the prayer in Gethsemane). Jesus does not prattle on about his relationship to God and how it feels. The Gospels record almost nothing "historical" about the years between his birth and his baptism and the start of his ministry. His life before that is shrouded in mystery, and while there are plenty of authors that speculate wildly about Jesus going to India or Egypt or doing magic mushrooms, there is no evidence for any of this. It is just speculation.

Why don't the Gospels give us the path Jesus followed to get where he did so we could just follow it?

There is, and only ever will be, one Jesus of Nazareth just like there is only one you. No one else can be you ever. So no one else can be Jesus.

Ever.

Jesus is Jesus and you are you. If it was as simple as copying Jesus' journey, reading the books he read, listening to the teachers he heard, we still would not be able to copy him. Whatever his journey was it is not known to us.

What is known is the end result. His journey was recognized as complete when he was baptized by John in the Jordan and the Abba proclaimed his pleasure and the Spirit in its fullness was sent upon him. From that point on we see Jesus doing two things: subtly challenging the religion and culture of his time and bringing a teaching about a new culture, the way of the reign of God.

When we begin at the proper starting point, the crucifixion, where all god concepts die, then and only then can we come to the life of Jesus to make any sense of his teaching. Consumer Christianity, whether conservative or liberal, has managed to vacate Jesus' teaching of any real significance. As we saw in chapter 3, they both misread Jesus' death, so it is little wonder that they in turn have made hash of his teaching.

What he taught and the event of the Passion are one and the same thing. It is all about forgiveness. Forgiveness is the Way, the Path we take to becoming human like Jesus and thus "divine" like Jesus. Jesus' call for us to journey with him is to take the same path he took, forgiving the sins of others and thus bringing healing and reconciliation. This is the only Path to human community as it is conceived of in the kingdom of God.

Since the Gospels begin not with an account of Jesus' spiritual journey to his baptism but with his ministry, it behooves us to ask why we think we can participate in his baptism and mission if we have not undergone a similar journey. If his journey ended with a proclamation of jubilee through the forgiveness of sins, through the healing of the poor, through the rejection of all economies of exchange whether religious, theological, social, or economic, then how can we possibly think we can get to where he arrived *if* we will not work backwards from his ministry to his culture and see where he diverged?

If we start with Jesus' mission and assume it is also our mission, we are undertaking an impossible journey, for we are not equipped to engage such a mission. As long as there are aspects of "power over," vestiges of the justification of violence, scapegoating practices or any form of recrimination (AKA "justice"), we cannot begin to undertake any ministry that is formed by Jesus.

Jesus was a pacifist whether you like it or not.

To have him incarnate in your life, to claim him as your master means you also will follow this path of nonresistance and forgiveness. There is no other way. This is the only way. Any other way is a Lie from Consumer Christianity.

More to the point: If Jesus is present to us by the Spirit, and if we affirm that God is one, how is it possible to have God present to us in any other form than that which we see in the life and teaching of Jesus?

If we have "died with Jesus" in his death, if we have been "raised with Jesus" in his resurrection, and if we have been "seated at the right hand of God" in Jesus' ascension, how could we possibly suppose that we are left in this life to follow a two-faced god, a god of both wrath and mercy, a god who loves and hates, a god like all the other gods which is what we do *not* see in the story of Jesus with the total, complete, and absolute forgiveness of the human species for bringing Death into the world?

The deception of Consumer Christianity is at its thickest at this point where the rubber meets the road, where we live our daily lives. Sure, Consumer Christianity says it teaches all about the death, resurrection, and ascension of Jesus. It claims to teach about how God's Spirit is in our lives but at every point it does its best to make sure that Jesus fades. It claims his teaching on peace and forgiveness is not realistic, it doesn't work for this world, or that it was not meant for this world but for some future dispensation. Both liberal and conservative Christian stores sell this merchandise.

The proof is in the pudding: when one looks out at the thousands of variations of the Christian Faith on offer at the Mall, one does not find a radical and total commitment to forgiveness, the only invincible power.

The proof is further seen in that the customers of the Mall, for all of their blustering and boasting of how they follow Jesus do not exhibit in their own groups or among themselves any actualization of forgiveness.

The opposite of forgiveness is Righteousness or Justice, always conceived from within an economy of exchange. Consumer Christianity preaches, teaches, lives, and follows a god who gets even, who balances scales, who makes sure every last drop of recompense and judgment is wrung from Divine Honor.

This god is an idol and this idol's son is none other than JeZeus.

Buyer beware.

Jesus promised his presence to his followers. Consumer Christianity has arrogated that promise to themselves *even as they reject his mission and message.* So you tell me, how is Jesus really present in modern American Consumer Christianity?

When we come to the gospel the first thing we notice is that Jesus only ever calls persons to follow him, never groups. Discipleship is not about what the group thinks or does; it is about listening to the singular voice of God found in Jesus.

Second, unlike Consumer Christianity with its fancy packaging, Jesus places a warning on discipleship: he says that if we begin this journey with him and look back wistfully at how much life seemed easier in the Mall, we are not worthy to follow him. He says that if we are called to follow him and consider that there are other things more important than that, we ought not to even begin the journey. He says to those who think discipleship is about health, wealth, glory, success, fame and fortune that following him will create displacement (Luke 9).

Third, as we noted in chapter 3, discipleship is all about forgiveness. Not just a little forgiveness but a forgiveness that knows no bounds, has no limits, and cannot do math. The disciple, like the master, forgives and forgives and forgives and forgives, even if someone hurts you 490 times during any given day (seventy times seven).

Jesus told a riddle about forgiveness that is just as mind-boggling today to Consumer Christianity as it was to those in his lifetime. In that little parable he speaks of a servant who was forgiven a huge debt, like $1,000,000; a debt so big it could never be repaid except for spending a lifetime in jail as recompense. This fella, now forgiven by the Big Boss, meets a fellow who owes him $1. He proceeds to demand repayment, as he has just been fired from his job. We all remember how the Boss responds. He tosses the poor sod into the clink, and there he remains unable to repay his debt with anything other than his time in the cell.

So shall it be for those so-called consumers of Christianity who claim that God forgives them but they do not have to forgive others.

If we trust that Jesus is present with us and that we follow him, then our lives will look more and more like his. If we claim he is compassionate when he forgives us but we do not forgive those who persecute us, how are we like him? If we claim to be loving but despise those who hurt us, how are we like him? If we claim that he is merciful, but we demand recompense for crimes and offenses and sins against us, how are we like him?

Forgiveness changes us at the deepest levels. When we forgive our enemies and those who hurt us we are God-like. When we hold people's sins against them, when we seek recompense and justice, we are god-like. These are the only two ways that exist in the universe.

Consumer Christianity wants you to have feel-good experiences whether they are personal or corporate. It seduces you into thinking that these experiences of belonging to a group or to a superhero god are the be-all and end-all of the Christian life. Discipleship teaches you *how* to suffer in this world for "in this world you will have tribulation."

Consumer Christianity justifies you when you defend your life; discipleship with Jesus justifies you when you give your life away.

Consumer Christianity winds you up and pulls your string so that all you can say is "Jesus didn't mean what he said about forgiving others." Discipleship with Jesus calls you to an unknown path, the path of peacemaking through forgiveness.

Consumer Christianity calls upon psychology, sociology, political theory, and every other discipline it can to compromise Jesus' teaching and render it impotent. Discipleship with Jesus takes Jesus at his word that trusting the Abba for one's existence is all that matters.

What does all of this have to do with incarnation?

The dogma of the incarnation is the assertion that God became human in Jesus of Nazareth. Christians have spent far too much time trying to sort out all of the philosophical (metaphysical) implications of this for 2,000 years. They have sought to relate the divinity of Jesus to his humanity in countless ways, most of them rather absurdly *because they have taken their definitions of "God" and "humanity" from anywhere else but the life of Jesus*. In their great error they make grandiose claims and condemn those who won't make similar ones.

It is impossible to speak of the incarnation of Jesus 2,000 years ago without at the same time speaking of the incarnation of Jesus today in his followers. Consumer Christianity would have you believe that it is indeed possible to do pie-in-the-sky-by-and-by thinking about all this as they covertly separate the God-human relationship from how Jesus lived and what he taught. Oh, they have all manner of high falutin' language they use, like *person, substance, being, ontology*, and the like—but nowhere are they willing to say that the same Jesus who lived and taught 2,000 years ago is the same Jesus who inhabits and orients our existence today.

Incarnation as a dogma is all about the way the Father of light and love redeems us and how by the Spirit sent from the Abba through the Son, so much so that the Spirit looks, speaks, and acts like Jesus, shapes us, molds us, and transforms us into his redemptive image. There is no disjunction between who Jesus is, what he does, and what he teaches.

There is no divide between Jesus' theology and his ethic; they are two sides of a coin. It is Jesus' "view of God" that reflects his ethic, for he grounds his mission in an apostolic office as one having been sent by God. To speak of divinity and humanity in Jesus must have as its complement the same speech about God coming into our lives and transfiguring them day by day so that we look more and more like the Son, the True Human, who has been given all authority.

In the Gospel incarnation is discipleship. Incarnation is not about some abstract equation of how Jesus could be 100 percent God and 100 percent human and still be just 100 percent total. Incarnation is not about speculative philosophical mind games. The Gospels really have no interest in *how* God became human; they are all focused on the type of human God became.

Thus, incarnation is discipleship.

This brings us to a further implication that is derived from Paul; the body of Jesus is still on the planet. He is incarnate in his disciples, those who have heard his question and answered his call to follow him. Just as we cannot speak of the Father and the Son without including the Spirit, so we cannot speak of Jesus without including his followers.

Jesus lives in his followers *by the Spirit*. He becomes enfleshed in our lives.

"How?" you ask. "How does this work out? What does this discipleship look like?"

The answer is shared by Paul in a letter written from prison to his followers in a Roman colony, Philippi. In the majestic hymn of Philippians 2:5–11 there is given us this intimate connection between incarnation and discipleship. It tells us how God as Son engages incarnation as discipleship, and Paul admonishes us to have the exact same mind-set.

He makes these "steps" explicit:

1. Although Jesus was in form as God, Jesus did not consider that equality with God either consisted of a thing to be grasped or held onto or to be the power to grasp such. Instead,
2. Jesus emptied himself. Of what? Christians get cute when they try to parse out which "divine attributes" he gave up and

which he kept. This is not about that. The Son emptied himself of any need to be a Self and that is all. The Son did this out of obedience to the Father; the Son only seeks the Abba's will. Thus the Son became a servant of the Abba.

3. As a servant of God he is first made human as all other humans and second is given a specific humanity; he becomes all of us as he becomes one of us.

4. Jesus humbled himself; he did not prance around saying "Lookee here! I'm Jesus, the great and powerful Messiah." Rather, he came as a laborer and allowed his journey as a human to take him where it took him, even to the death which came to all humans. But more than that:

5. He humbled himself to die the horror and terror and shame of a Roman cross. He trusted his Abba all the way down. He trusted that he doing the Abba's will even as he walked the dark and forboding canyons of the shadow of Death.

Let us summarize. Incarnation as discipleship consists of:

1. Letting go.
2. Becoming a willing vessel for the Father to inhabit.
3. Accepting that one is totally consumed with the Abba's love and that circumstances are no indicator of that love.
4. To trust the Abba even when one is cast into the outer darkness (according to the world) thus "letting go" of the attempt to give meaning to one's life and trust the Abba to weave a good and beautiful tapestry. It is the awareness that Death is not the final word and has no authority as a word or power over us. It is the state of shalom.

We have seen over and over again the importance of the act of forgiveness in Jesus' death and its implications for our thinking about God and ourselves and others. Jesus' path of discipleship is the path of the True Human, the Human totally given over to the Father, a path vindicated in the resurrection and a path that continues to be lived by Jesus in his followers. Thus, speaking of the incarnation of Jesus both in terms of his historical ministry and his ongoing ministry through his followers, it can be seen that knowing God is knowing Jesus and knowing Jesus occurs when the call to follow him is heeded.

You cannot know Jesus apart from following him and you cannot know the Father apart from Jesus.

We know where this journey begins: at the cross, and we know where it will end in our life, as cross-carrying people. Now before you freak out, don't go thinking I am trying to hype suffering. No way.

To carry a cross is another way of saying that you will, like Jesus, forgive those who hurt you. The only thing that stops any one of us from forgiving others is our belief that God has an economy of exchange, a tit-for-tat struggle within God's soul between mercy and justice. We have seen that *that* god concept is shown to be a Lie at Calvary. Unlike the voice of Abel, the victim who seeks recrimination or justice, a voice we also hear all through Israel's Songbook (the Psalms), Jesus' voice is of another order. His blood is better than Abel's because although Abel's blood had a voice (unlike the victims of myth), Jesus' voice has nothing to do with balancing cosmic scales through any notion of "justice."

Forgiveness flowed through the veins of Jesus while on earth and now flows through our veins as he dwells in us and we follow him. We are the light of the world even as he was historically the light of his world. We have all been included in him, even Christians, but out addiction to the merchandise of the Mall of Consumer Christianity has until now prohibited us from seeing this.

But now we see. His path is clear.

We know where it goes and we also know that the end of Jesus' story was not The End nor will the end of our historical story be

The End of us. We see how God has included us all by placing us all at the cross as Jesus' persecutors. We hear the gospel that we are all forgiven *even as we commit the very act itself*. We are invited to follow the risen Jesus and just as he allowed the Abba to incarnate God's self in his life, so too we create space daily for Jesus to inhabit our hours, minutes, and seconds.

We take no view of ourselves. Successful? Not successful? It doesn't matter: these are not categories used in discipleship. We do not allow the measure of others to determine our value or worth, nor do we listen to the voices in our heads that denigrate us and devalue us. We trust that all our value and worth is given us by the Abba. If you, even though you are far from perfect, know how to give value and worth to your offspring, how much more does the Father of light and the Mother Spirit love "their" children?

Followers of Jesus are those who have transcended the persecutor-victim dualism that governs the planet and all human religion. They are neither persecutors nor are they victims after the manner of Abel.

Followers of Jesus are victims of a different order.

You will recall that in the chapter on crucifixion I mentioned that there is an intentionality to being a victim in the manner Jesus was a victim. Let us be clear: Jesus did not choose to be a victim, nor did he intentionally provoke authorities so they would make him one. Jesus avoided trouble this way all the time. He was not a provocateur (the action in the Temple was so small a prophetic act that word never reached the Roman guard of a civil disturbance. It cannot be used to justify social violence or disturbance. It did not have that sort of [anachronistic] political function for Jesus).

Jesus' intentionality is manifest in his orientation, even as he criticized the religious leaders of his day and the religious institutions of his upbringing. This exact same intentionality is manifest in his critique of the Christian religion today as was his historical criticism of how the Jewish faith was practiced by many of those in authority.

Jesus calls upon his followers to forgive the Christian leaders who persecute them, who cast them out, who smear their reputations. He calls upon his followers to bless them and forgive them, for it is only in dying that life comes forth.

Our lives are just seeds and until a grain of seed falls into the ground and dies, it remains . . .

A seed.

However, when it is planted the conditions of the soil and the changing weather break that seed open, and life springs forth.

Cross.

Resurrection.

"They killed us and they buried us; they didn't know we were seeds."

The world is not saved through justice or righteousness or holiness or vengeance or retribution.

It was saved once for all through forgiveness. It is the invincible power of forgiveness that the follower of Jesus possesses. When the follower of Jesus dies, they not do not carry any of their "sin" into death, for it has been forgiven.

They also carry no one else's sin with them into death, for the others' sin too has been forgiven.

Abel took Cain's sin with him into death, which is why his voice could only ever cry out for justice. Jesus did not take any of our sin against him into death and so could come back to life as our peace. The risen Jesus can announce "Peace" because he has taken no offense; he and his Abba have kept no accounts, no records, no ledgers.

All of our thinking coalesces around the cross and forgiveness, the true and final revelation of the character of God. If you are in a theological frame of mind you will have observed that all of the doctrines implicitly or explicitly mentioned take the cross of Jesus of Nazareth as their starting point. One cannot speak of any one "doctrine" in isolation from any other, but if you go to the Mall you will find all doctrines arranged as sections and none of them oriented to the cross. This is how they confuse you.

The gospel has a center from which all thinking, living, and relating stems and flows.

Jesus of Nazareth, True Human, Son sent from the Abba, dead at our hands.

Risen Jesus, bringer of peace and love and light.

Present Jesus, counselor, advocate, teacher, master.

Incarnate Jesus . . . in our flesh.

If you have become dissatisfied with the dust and ashes you have been eating from the Christian table, if you are weary of believing in a god who is beating you down or that does not care . . .

There is a table set for you and a Host that invites you to shed your worries and your burdens and your fears and says "Come, eat."

Just as he did in the first century, so now Jesus is calling humans to follow him on the true and living path, the path of peace and reconciliation, the only path that leads to the reign of God:

The path of forgiveness.

As we learn to walk this path we follow Jesus into God's future, a future where the lion lays down with the lamb, where the persecutor is embraced by the victim. This is a future where there is no predator or prey for everything is given life in itself and no longer needs to consume anything but lives from the light of love alone.

And *that* will suffice for all of eternity.

CONCLUSION

A Two Chart Primer On How To Read The Bible

The structure of the Christian life is the exact opposite of that life of Jesus as we find it in the Gospels. The Gospels begin with the sending of Jesus into the world, his life downward to the cross, and then up again through resurrection to ascension. That is, Jesus' story looks like a capital letter U.

The Christian life however is the exact opposite for it begins at the bottom with crucifixion, moves up through resurrection and ascension, only to move back down again through the sending of the Spirit into incarnation (that is, Jesus incarnate in us by the Spirit, otherwise known as ecclesiology or the doctrine of the church). We mess things up when we start at the bottom and ascend, rather than starting at the top and descending. Both are found in the apostolic writings. An example of the first is Philippians 2:5–11, an example of the second is John 1:51.

In this book I have come down very hard on Consumer Christianity, but I would not want you think I am dismissing the Christian faith "tradition," for in that rich and plentiful stream are many writers and thinkers and pietists, monks and nuns, mystics and lay people of all stripes who have heard the gospel and have left us their witness.

The Christian tradition, like the Bible itself, contains two streams, that of religion and that of revelation, and both streams run throughout both biblical Testaments and on into the major world religions of Judaism and Christianity.

Where Protestantism has gotten it all wrong in all of its expressions is the failure to adequately take the crucified Jesus as the means by which all interpretation of all reality and life and texts must be done. Protestantism has tended to magnify all out of proportion Scripture, tradition, experience, or reason. Just examine any Protestant tradition found in Consumer Christianity and you will find one of these four is all out of whack with the other three. Now the Wesleyans can be credited with this fourfold model of how we do theology, but it failed (particularly in the American Episcopal and Methodist Churches) in that each category was given definition from within a closed box, a box that had already turned God into all the other gods of our imagination and nightmares. Rather than allowing the person and teaching of Jesus to be the mean, norm, standard, or canon, Protestants have as a rule domesticated Jesus and his teaching. Consumer Christianity locks the gate to the gospel so no one can enter in; Jesus unlocks it so we can all escape the Mall!

In the second edition of my book *The Jesus Driven Life* I contended for the benefits of this fourfold model of Scripture, tradition, experience, and reason but reconceived in terms of Jesus. The following diagram will help you to see what happens when we allow the gospel to create its own meaning instead of trying to get Jesus to fit into our box.

How do we know God?

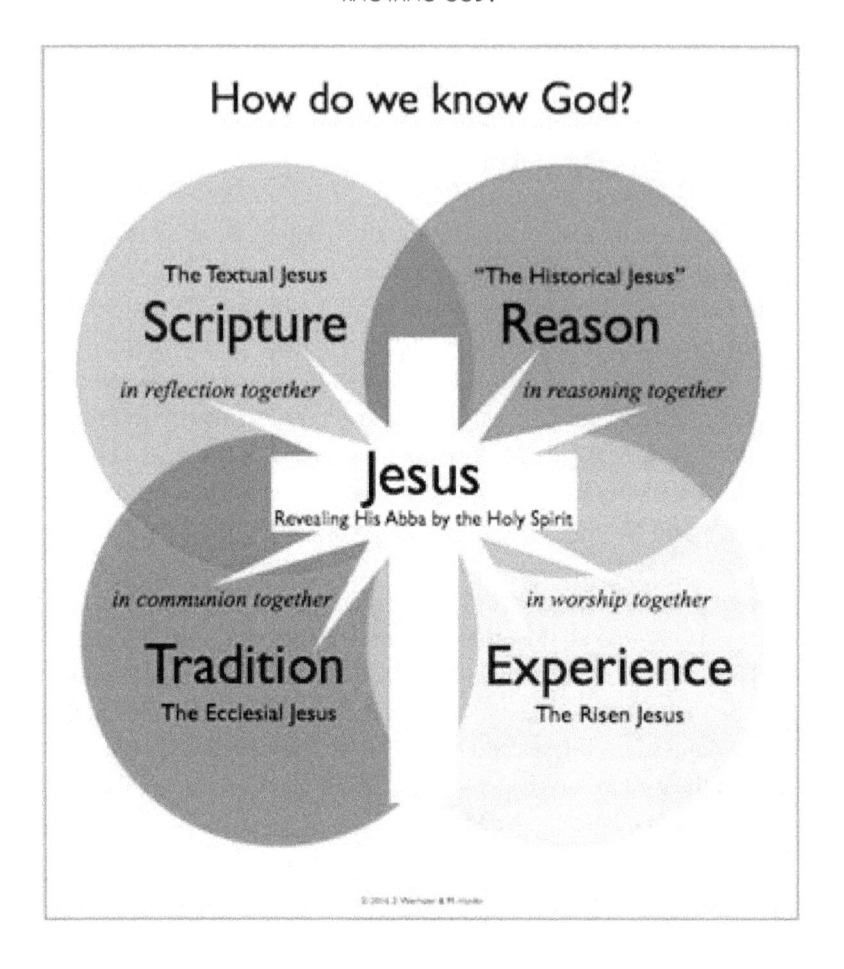

Scripture — The Textual Jesus — *in reflection together*

Reason — "The Historical Jesus" — *in reasoning together*

Jesus — Revealing His Abba by the Holy Spirit

Tradition — The Ecclesial Jesus — *in communion together*

Experience — The Risen Jesus — *in worship together*

The explanation of this chart comes from my book *The Jesus Driven Life*:

In the eighteenth century John Wesley was credited with using four different sources to do theology: Scripture, reason, tradition, and experience. You can draw a square and place each of these terms in each of the four corners. Now each of these categories needs to be defined. What is reason? What is experience? What part of the tradition shall we recognize as authoritative? Do we all agree on what constitutes the biblical canon? Each of these has been discussed and debated from the early church to the present. What I would like to do is to "christologize" them, that is, make each one Jesus centered. So take your square and next to each one write:

Scripture = The Textual Jesus
Reason = "The Historical Jesus"
Tradition = The Ecclesial Jesus
Experience = The Risen Jesus

The chronological order of these for the early church was experience, tradition, Scripture, reason. They are not necessarily our chronological frame. We may come to Jesus through any one the four corners and it is Jesus we encounter. But if we remain in one corner to the exclusion of the others we will not know Jesus fully, for he is manifested not just in our experience, not just in our tradition, not just in the Bible, and not just in our academic discourse about him. He is known best when all four are engaged.

First is the Risen Jesus. This is our personal experience of the presence of Jesus in our lives by the gift of the Holy Spirit.

Second is the Ecclesial Jesus. This is Jesus as we may know him through the teaching of others who have gone before us and especially as we gather together as the body of Jesus (Christ) today. This recognizes that no understanding of Jesus is only private but that every understanding is interpersonal or interrelational.

Third is the Textual Jesus. This is the recognition that each of the four Gospels paints a different portrait of Jesus, that the writers of the Gospels have a theological agenda when they write, that we may discern that agenda and that we may learn from it how they understood Jesus.

Fourth is the "Historical Jesus." You will note that this last is in quotes. That is because the so-called "Historical Jesus" is a creature of academic imagination. It is the attempt to discern who Jesus was in the context of his culture and environment and which sayings of his can be considered historically credible or authentic. The quotation marks indicate the changing nature of this Jesus. As we learn more about second Temple Judaism and the various groups and worldviews and theologies of his time, so also we see Jesus differently.

Each of these is necessary for us to come to a well-rounded and more complete view of Jesus. No single aspect alone suffices. Not even two or three suffice. Some would say that we do not need the "Historical Jesus" but the problem here is that the Jesus they end up speaking about loses his humanity and connection to a particular space and time. This is a form of Christian Gnosticism. Some scholars, on the other hand, would virtually tell us that anything but the "Historical Jesus" is baloney and so they miss out on the fact that Jesus is known beyond just the intellect. Some (so-called) "Historical Jesus" portraits are just as suspect as those who would claim a purely "Spirit-inspired" knowledge of him.

All four together are necessary and can function as a control on the other three at any given time. How then do we know Jesus? We know him in worship together, in study together, in reflection together, and in reasoning together. We know him together as his body. Those who would focus on one extreme or another will never know the beauty, the reality, the joy that is Jesus, Lord of all creation, reconciler of all creation and redeemer of all creation.

If you are serious about following Jesus you cannot write off the Christian faith, for it is a religion in travail. It is a religion stuck between myth and gospel, like much modern religion. There is great wisdom in the tradition and it must be refined and the dross drawn off so the pure gold remains. One can retire to almost any century in the Christian tradition and there find witnesses to the gospel of peace as it is found in Jesus. Many times these persons were unknown during their lifetime; others only gained any public awareness these past several hundred years. From the second-century Epistle to Diognetus to the twentieth-century *Discipleship* by Dietrich Bonhoeffer, the Christ of the gospel has been proclaimed and at the heart of that proclamation is the non-retributive character of Jesus and the One he follows, imitates, and hears: the Father.

Conversely, if you only know Jesus in your head, if you only know things about him but have not undergone the experience of being crucified, of "undergoing God" as James Alison puts it, then you are not yet a theologian. To follow Jesus is to put real flesh and blood to his message of peace and forgiveness, and this means just as he lived then, so he lives now in us.

None of the fourfold elements is in and of themselves authoritative; they all bear witness to Jesus, the forgiving revelation of God.

Up to this point I have sought to stay away from all technical language and wish to continue to do so. However, if you wish to be able to read the Bible as Jesus read his Jewish Scriptures it is necessary to be able to distinguish revelation from religion in the Bible. This can be done by just asking one question:

Which voice is speaking?

In light of God's revelation having to do with our persecutory models of religion, it is the perspective of the Victim that alone provides revelation. However, I do not mean victims in general, for victims fall into one of three groups. There is first of all the victim of myth; that victim, when the story is told, deserved everything they had coming. For example, one of the more pure instances of this kind of myth in the Bible is in Joshua 7. A mythic or religious reading would conclude with the text that Achan was indeed guilty. A gospel reading of the text would perceive that the community has scapegoated Achan and covered it up. A gospel reading of this text would see the figure of Jesus in Achan; a mythic reading of the text would see God in the community's decision.

Most victims found in ancient mythologies that describe in symbolic-metaphoric terms the origination of a culture's religion and rise are guilty. America has its own share of myths, from the justification of killing witches in Puritan Massachusetts to the lynching of African Americans in nineteenth-century Alabama or gay men in Wisconsin in the twentieth century. When you read a story where the guilt of the victim is clear for all to see and the righteousness of the community is on display in their legitimate casting out of the victim, you have myth.

The Jewish tradition was the first religion to make a break with this. Revelation comes through in the Jewish Scriptures, for here the voice of the victim is heard. Abel's blood cries out from the ground and God hears it. The persecutors can no longer hide; they are exposed. The singers of Israel have plenty of songs (Psalms) lamenting their situation and asking God to redeem them, often seeking God's vengeance and/or justice. This is a different type of victim than the victim of myth inasmuch as this victim is able to voice their innocence or anger or usually both. This is "the victim in travail." This victim is not muted by myth, inasmuch as they have a voice, but this victim has not yet moved to gospel where forgiveness reigns. This victim is recriminatory, vengeful, angry and will by all means have satisfaction.

The move made by God in the Gospel is to break out of the eye-for-an-eye mentality (which we called an economy of exchange) and into that reality, the only reality that could bend sin and death to itself and thus overcome them: forgiveness.

Jesus is the forgiving Victim.

Once again we are back to the question that prompts this insight: "Why do you persecute me?"

And once again we are reminded that as we killed God, God was in Christ forgiving us the whole way down. In the gospel all recriminations have evaporated, all sin forgiven, all law eradicated, all threats blown away, all possibility of vengeance discounted.

GOD WAS IN CHRIST RECONCILING THE WORLD TO GOD'S SELF.

Revelation comes into the very structuring mechanism that we humans have created as we became civilized, as we formed groups, as we learned to cooperate in the hunt. That mechanism is human sacrifice. While most of us today would contend that we in fact do not commit human sacrifice, the fact is that we all do. We do not have to be some evil occultist killing women and children on an unholy altar; we can do it on Sunday mornings from a beautiful clean stage or a sanitized altar when we rail and screech at those whom we are sure God hates because we hate them.

This is the whole point of the Eucharist: to give us an alternative ritual where we recognize our propensity to sacrifice others (through thought, word, or deed) and whereby having named ourselves as blameworthy persecutors, we find ourselves in a forgiving relationship to the Divine Victim whose flesh we have consumed. The Eucharist then becomes the ritual that sustains us as we go out into the world and give our life away to the world, let them consume us, and we seek forgiveness for them.

Forgiveness is invincible.

Here is a diagram that illustrates this:

The Voices of Religion and Revelation: A Girardian Hermeneutic

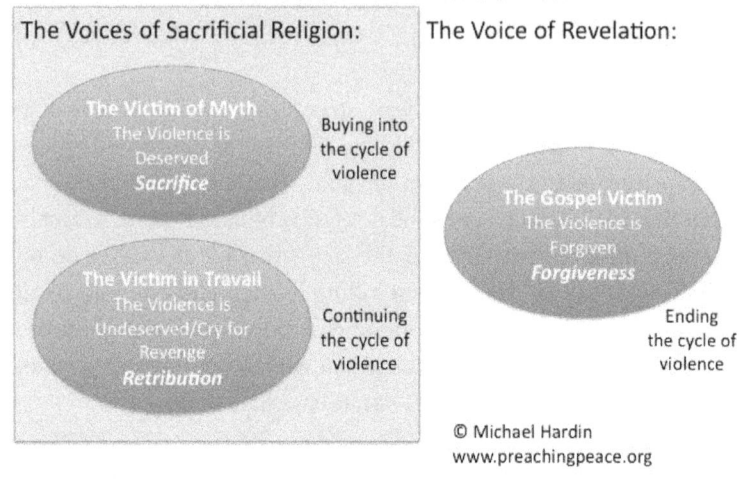

The Voices of Sacrificial Religion:

The Victim of Myth
The Violence is Deserved
Sacrifice

Buying into the cycle of violence

The Victim in Travail
The Violence is Undeserved/Cry for Revenge
Retribution

Continuing the cycle of violence

The Voice of Revelation:

The Gospel Victim
The Violence is Forgiven
Forgiveness

Ending the cycle of violence

© Michael Hardin
www.preachingpeace.org

In a nutshell, what I am proposing in this little book is this: Evangelical Protestant Christianity and all her step-children read the Bible *through the lens of the persecutor* and creates all manner of victims. They take the position of Caiaphas that it is better that one die than the group perish. Liberal Protestant Christianity reads the Bible *through the lens of the retributive blood of Abel*, demanding all manner of reparations for injustices perceived and real. Consumer Christianity is both of these; it is sacrificial religion and it is *not* the gospel.

Both liberal and conservative are contiguous religious readings, which is why the Mall of Consumer Christianity, for all of the infighting between the stores, really only carries one brand of product, that of religion dressed up in the language of the gospel. But it is really not the gospel at all. This also explains why neither side can get along with the other; they are both battling for rights to be the true religion when both are still in the box of sacrificial religion. This is the box that always finds room for coercion and makes a way for violence to be justified, whether in theology or ethics. That is all people in this box know.

Followers of Jesus, like Paul, have been reoriented by God to the forgiving Victim and thus are the only ones who can make any claim to knowing God.

Jesus asked a question during his lifetime of his disciples and it is the same question asked of every one who would follow him . . .

"Who do you say I am?"

And he calls to each and every one . . .

"Come, follow me."

What say you?

Resources from Michael Hardin

"American Protestant Reception of Girard." In *Handbook on Mimetic Theory*, edited by James Alison and Wolfgang Palaver, 225–32. New York: Palgrave Macmillan, 2017.

"The Authority of Scripture: A Pietist Perspective." *The Covenant Quarterly*, vol. 49, no. 1, 3–12.

Compassionate Eschatology. Edited by Michael Hardin and Ted Grimsrud. Eugene, OR: Cascade, 2011.

"Do Clergy Foster Co-Dependence?" *The Journal of Ministry in Addiction and Recovery*, vol. 2, no. 1 (1995) n.p.

"Hell: The Final Refuge of Sacrificial Religion." In *Hellrazed!*, edited by Kevin Miller, 83–92. Kimberley: Kevin Miller XI, 2017.

The Jesus Driven Life. Lancaster, PA: JDL, 2010, 2013. Translated into Korean by Hyun Hur (Seoul: Daejanggan, 2015). Translated into Spanish by Ricardo Garcia Reyes (Lancaster: JDL, 2016).

"Mimesis and Dominion: The Dynamics of Violence and the Imitation of Christ in Maximus Confessor." *St Vladimir's Theological Quarterly*, vol. 36, no. 4, 373–86.

Mimetic Theory and Biblical Interpretation. Cascade Companions. Eugene, OR: Cascade, 2017.

"Mimetic Theory and Christian Theology in the Twenty-First Century." In *For Rene Girard: Essays in Friendship and Truth*, edited by Sandor Goodhart, et al., 265–72. East Lansing, MI: Michigan State University Press, 2009.

Peace Be With You: The Church's Benediction Amid Violent Empires. Edited by Sharon L. Baker and Michael Hardin. Telford: Cascadia, 2010. Published in South Africa by ANISA (Pietermaritzburg, 2012).

"Practical Reflections on Nonviolent Atonement." In *Violence, Desire and the Sacred Vol. 2: René Girard and Sacrifice in Life, Love, and Literature*, edited by Joel Hodge, Scott Cowdell and Chris Fleming, 247–58. Notre Dame, IN: University of Notre Dame Press, 2014.

"Prophecy and Apocalypse: Native American Prophecy & the Mimetic Theory." Presented to the Colloquium on Violence and Religion, Riverside, CA June 2008; published in *Compassionate Eschatology*, 155–70.

Reading the Bible with Rene Girard. Edited and with an Introduction by Michael Hardin. Lancaster, PA: JDL, 2016. Translated into Spanish by Ricardo Garcia Reyes (Lancaster: JDL, 2016). Translated into Korean by Ellul Yongha Bae (Daejanggan: 2016).

"Reflections on the Spirituality of Søren Kierkegaard." *The Scottish Journal of Theology*, vol. 45 (1992) 325–40.

"Responses." In *Understanding Spiritual Warfare*, edited by James Beilby and Paul Eddy, 112–15, 158–62, 299–203. Grand Rapids: Baker Academic, 2012.

Stricken by God? Nonviolent Identification and the Victory of Christ. Edited by Brad Jersak and Michael Hardin. Grand Rapids: Eerdmans, 2007.

"Theological Existence Today: Identity Politics and the Gospel." In *Clarion Journal of Spirituality*, August 28, 2017. www.clarion-journal.com.

"A Theological Justification for the Anonymity of God." *The Journal of Ministry in Addiction and Recovery*, vol. 1, no. 2 (1994) 3–22.

"The Trinity as Hermeneutic: A Pietist Perspective." *The Covenant Quarterly*, vol. 45, no. 1 (1994) 47–68.

"The Twelve Steps and Christian Spirituality." *The Journal of Ministry in Addiction and Recovery*, vol. 1, no. 1, n.p.

"Violence: Rene Girard and the Recovery of Early Christian Perspectives." *Brethren Life and Thought*, vol. 37, no. 2 (2000) 103–19.

Walking with Grandfather: A Skeptic's Journey to Spirituality. Lancaster, PA: JDL, 2014.

My website www.preachingpeace.org has a plethora of free video series, essays, ebooks, and podcasts that explore in further depth how to read the Bible as Jesus read the Bible and how to engage the discipline of Christian theological thinking and living. There is also a Lectionary Commentary on the Gospels and Epistles available for those who preach and teach. I also have two YouTube channels (Preaching Peace and Michael Hardin) and you can find me on Facebook as the Dude of Theology.

And yes, the Dude abides.